Snežana Stefanović

Learn Serbian Cyrillic

Textbook

3. Edition

Serbian Reader

Introduction

The book „Learn Serbian Cyrillic" is a textbook for learning Cyrillic script, which is in use in Serbia in its three forms: as block letters – *štampana slova*, as block letters in cursive – *štampana kosa slova*, and as written letters – *pisana slova*.

The textbook contains didactically prepared exercises: the letters of the Cyrillic script are practiced in groups and consolidated through writing and reading exercises as well as short texts in dialogue and narrative form. The more demanding passages can be easily understood with the help of the English translation. Words without translation are just as easy to understand due to their similarity to English words.

In terms of language level, all exercises and texts are at language level A1 = novice low/mid/high: the learner has a simple vocabulary and with the help of the English translations can easily understand the texts and exercises.

At the end of the book you will find „Key to Exercises" for longer text exercises that are translated into English.

When you come to a writing exercise, please write down your exercises in a notebook or on a piece of paper. This way, your exercises will remain clear and can be repeated as often as you like. The symbol below indicates a writing exercise.

a) Alphabet in Latin Script – latinica

Serbian is officially written in the Cyrillic script as of 2006, but the Latin script is learned in school as well as used in the media, public administration, and public signage.

Since the book „Learn Serbian Cyrillic" is intended for language level A1 = Novice Low/Mid/High, it is useful – before learning Cyrillic – to know or learn the alphabet with Serbian sounds. So first an overview of the alphabet in Latin letters.

Typical Serbian sounds/letters are: Č, Ć, Đ, DŽ, Lj, Nj, Š, Ž.

A, a	B, b	C, c	Č, č	Ć, ć
		=	=	=
		like **ts** (cats)	like **ch** (chocolate)	*like Ital.* **Ci**ao!
D, d	Đ, đ	Dž, dž	E, e	F, f
	=	=	=	
	like **j** (juice)	*like* **j** – **J**ohn	like **e** (men)	
G, g	H, h	I, i	J, j	K, k
=	=	=	=	=
like **g** (good)	like **h** (hot)	like **e** (east)	like **y** (you)	like **k** (king)
L, l	Lj, lj	M, m	N, n	Nj, nj
	=			=
	like **li** (million)			like **ni** (onion)
O, o	P, p	R, r	S, s	Š, š
=			=	=
like **o** (door)			ß (wie Ro**ß**)	like **sh** (she)
T, t	U, u	V, v	Z, z	Ž, ž
		=	=	=
		like **v** (victory)	like **z** (zoo)	like **su** (leisure)

b) Alphabet in Cyrillic Script – ćirilica

The Cyrillic script – **ćirilica** – has three types of letters:

1) block letters – *štampana slova*

2) block letters in cursive – *štampana kosa slova*

3) written letters – *pisana slova.*

Ad 1)

Block letters – *štampana slova* are used in printed materials – books, newspapers, etc. – and are generally not used in writing.

Ad 2)

When **block letters** are written **in cursive** – *štampana kosa slova,* there are a few differences from block letters: at five letters, and only lowercase.

Ad 3)

When writing, the **written letters** – *pisana slova* are used. The difference between writtten letters and block letters is only six letters.

In school – and also in this book – block letters are learned first, then block letters in cursive, and finally written letters.

Block Letters – *štampana slova*

A a = А а	Dž dž = Џ џ	I i = И и	N n = Н н	Š š = Ш ш
B b = Б б	Đ đ = Ђ ђ	J j = J j	Nj nj = Њ њ	T t = Т т
C c = Ц ц	E e = Е е	K k = К к	O o = О о	U u = У у
Č č = Ч ч	F f = Ф ф	L l = Л л	P p = П п	V v = В в
Ć ć = Ћ ћ	G g = Г г	Lj lj = Љ љ	R r = Р р	Z z = З з
D d = Д д	H h = X x	M m = М м	S s = С с	Ž ž = Ж ж

The alphabet used in Serbia - the sequence of letters - is called „azbuka" and differs from the Latin alphabet:

a, b, v, g, d, đ, e, ž, z, i, j, k, l, lj, m, n, nj, o, p, r, s, t, ć, u, f, h, c, č, dž, š

In our book we do not use „**azbuka**", but the Latin alphabetical order. The reason is to facilitate the learning of Cyrillic. Using the letters in the order of „**azbuka**" plays a role when looking up a Serbian-Serbian dictionary, where the sequence of letters is given in azbuka order. Now, the use of a Serbian-Serbian dictionary usually comes into play at higher language levels, not at the beginning of learning Serbian.

Letters: a, o, e, m, t, k, j

Block Letters – *štampana slova*

A a = A a	Dž dž = Џ џ	I i = И и	N n = Н н	Š š = Ш ш
B b = Б б	Đ đ = Ђ ђ	J j = Ј ј	Nj nj = Њ њ	T t = Т т
C c = Ц ц	E e = E e	K k = К к	O o = O o	U u = У у
Č č = Ч ч	F f = Ф ф	L l = Л л	P p = П п	V v = В в
Ć ć = Ћ ћ	G g = Г г	Lj lj = Љ љ	R r = Р р	Z z = З з
D d = Д д	H h = Х х	M m = М м	S s = С с	Ž ž = Ж ж

As you've noticed, there are seven letters that are similar to English:
A a, O o, E e, M м, T т, K к, J j

Here are a few exercises with only these letters.

1. Write in Cyrillic in your notebook or on a piece of paper and read aloud! – 
Napiši na ćirilici i čitaj glasno!

mama (*mom*)

tata (*dad*)

jako (*ver*)

tamo (*there, over there*)

ako (*when, if*)

tek (*first, just*)

koji (*which - male*)

kome (*whom*)

tako (*so*)

kako (*how, as*)

jaje (*egg*)

ja (*I*)

ko (*who*)

moj (*my*)

koja (*which - female*)

jeka (*echo*)

je (*is*)

meta (*target*)

kej (*kai*)

motka (*rod, bar*)

jato (*swarm*)

jama (*pit*)

moja (*my - female*)

tama (*darkness*)

kajak (*kayak*)

mek (*soft*)

tok (*run, course*)

mak (*poppy*)

2. Write in Cyrillic in your notebook or on a piece of paper and read aloud! – Napiši na ćirilici i čitaj glasno!

mom

How?

very

I

my (male)

Which (male)?

Whom?

first, just

dad

So.

there

Who?

kai

Which (female)?

when, if

egg

3. Write in Cyrillic in your notebook or on a piece of paper and read aloud! – Napiši na ćirilici i čitaj glasno!

Personal names:

Tomo

Mato

Kata

Maja

Momo

Tom

Matej

Kaja

**4. Write in Cyrillic in your notebook or on a piece of paper and read aloud! –
Napiši na ćirilici i čitaj glasno!** 

Kaja je mama. (Kaja is a mom.)

Ko je tata? (Who ist a dad?)

Tomo je tata. (Tomo ist a dad.)

Kako je Maja? (How is Maja?)

Ko je Momo? (Who is Momo?)

Moj kajak je mek. (My kayak is soft.)

Moja Kata je tamo. (My Kata is over there.)

Koja Maja? (Which Maja?)

Letters: r, d, b, g

Mark letters you already know! – Obeleži slova koja već poznaješ!

A a = A a	Dž dž = Џ џ	I i = И и	N n = Н н	Š š = Ш ш
B b = Б б	Đ đ = Ђ ђ	J j = J j	Nj nj = Њ њ	T t = Т т
C c = Ц ц	E e = E e	K k = К к	O o = O o	U u = У у
Č č = Ч ч	F f = Ф ф	L l = Л л	P p = П п	V v = В в
Ć ć = Ћ ћ	G g = Г г	Lj lj = Љ љ	R r = Р р	Z z = З з
D d = Д д	H h = Х х	M m = М м	S s = С с	Ž ž = Ж ж

The following letters that are learned are:

Latin script	R r	D d	B b	G g
Cyrillic Block Letters	**Р р**	**Д д**	**Б б**	**Г г**

1. Write in Cyrillic in your notebook or on a piece of paper and read aloud! – Napiši na ćirilici i čitaj glasno!

komet (*comet*) = комет

koga (*who - acc.*) кога

gde (*where*)

taj (*this*)

Beograd

deda (*grandpa*)

tada (*then*)

more (*sea*)

draga (*dear - feminine*)

beba (*baby*)

dama (*lady*)

kada (*when*)

drama	treba (*needs*)
grad (*town*)	kratak (*short - masculine*)
kome (*whom*)	baba (*grandma*)
metar	aerodrom (*airport*)
boem (*bohemian*)	dobar (*good*)
toga (*this - acc.masculine*)	ker (*dog*)
boja (*color*)	Kaja
gaj (*grove*)	dok (*while*)
magma	obrok (*portion*)
jod (*iodine*)	Mara
gora (*mountain*)	Bog (*God*)
geg (*Gag*)	doba (*season*)
Tara	beta
bor (*fir tree*)	Dara
tera	tema (*theme*)
domet (range)	rok (*deadline*)
deo (*part*)	mrak (*darkness*)
jad (*misery*)	grm (*bush*)
tome (*to this - dat. masculine*)	batak (*chicken leg*)
rado (*gladly*)	kratka (*short – feminine*)
bager (*digger*)	Magda
ideja (*idea*)	to (*this*)

2. Write in Latin in your notebook or on a piece of paper and read aloud! – Napiši na latinici i čitaj glasno!

мама, тата, баба, деда (*mom, dad, grandma, grandpa*)

мој аеродром (*my airport*)

моја тема (*my theme*)

моја беба (*my baby*)

кратка драма (*a short play*)

То је мој оброк. (*This is my food portion.*)

Дара треба море. (*Dara needs the sea.*)

Београд је мој град. (*Belgrade is my city.*)

Како је мама? (*How´s mom?*)

Како је тата? (*How´s dad?*)

Где је Мара? (*Where´s Mara?*)

3. Write in Cyrillic in your notebook or on a piece of paper and translate! – Napiši na ćirilici i prevedi!

Draga! Kako si?

Ja sam dobro.

Kako je beba?

Gde je moj tata?

To je dobra ideja.

Gde je more?

Tamo je more.

Gde je Mara?

Ko to treba?

Ja to trebam.

Letters: h, l, u

Mark letters you already know! – Obeleži slova koja već poznaješ!

A a = A a	Dž dž = Џ џ	I i = И и	N n = Н н	Š š = Ш ш
B b = Б б	Đ đ = Ђ ђ	J j = J j	Nj nj = Њ њ	T t = Т т
C c = Ц ц	E e = E e	K k = К к	O o = О o	U u = У y
Č č = Ч ч	F f = Ф ф	L l = Л л	P p = П п	V v = В в
Ć ć = Ћ ћ	G g = Г г	Lj lj = Љ љ	R r = Р p	Z z = З з
D d = Д д	H h = Х x	M m = М м	S s = C c	Ž ž = Ж ж

Now we practice the other letters:

Latin script	H h	L l	U u
Cyrillic block letters	**Х x**	**Л л**	**У y**

1. Write in Cyrillic in your notebook or on a piece of paper and read aloud! – Napiši na ćirilici i čitaj glasno!

hotel (*hotel*)

mleko (*milk*)

tu (*here*)

luk (*onion*)

hrabar (*brave*)

rame (*shoulder*)

guma (*rubber*)

let (*flight*)

lekar (*doctor*)

kuda (*where to*)

led (*ice*)

Ratko

lakat (*elbow*)

beo (*white*)

rum (*rum*)

hala (*hall*)

duga (*rainbow*)

dur (*major - music*)

klub (*club*)

lama (*llama*)

lutka (*doll*)

buka (*noise*)

Goga

rub (*edge*)

bubamara (*ladybug*)

duh (*spirit*)

rat (*war*)

mera (*measure*)

u (*in*)

kula (*tower*)

mol (*minor - music*)

Lela

hram (*temple*)

Homer

lom (*break*)

hod (*walk*)

roda (*stork*)

lug (*floodplain forest*)

lira (*lyre*)

letak (*pamphlet*)

2. Write in Cyrillic in your notebook or on a piece of paper and read aloud! – Napiši na ćirilici i čitaj glasno!

Lara je moja beba. (*Lara is my baby.*)

To je jako dobar hotel. (*This is a very good hotel.*)

Tu je bela kula. (*Here is the white tower.*)

Moj lakat je kratak. (*My elbow is short.*)

Mleko je belo. (*Milk is white.*)

Boba je mala. (*Boba is small.*)

Moj lekar je dobar. (*My doctor is good.*)

Moj tata je hrabar. (*My dad is brave.*)

Moja lutka je meka. (*My doll is soft.*)

Ko je ta dama? (*Who is this lady?*)

Gde je luk? (*Where´s the onion?*)

Gde je klub? (*Where´s the club?*)

Kuda? – Tamo. (*Where to? – There.*)

Kako je Bora? (*How´s Bora?*)

Gde je rum? (*Where is rum?*)

Ratko je u hotelu. (*Ratko is in the hotel.*)

Ta ideja je dobra i hrabra. (*This idea is good and brave.*)

Gora Tara je mala? (*The mountain Tara is small?*)

Borka treba dobar obrok. (*Borka needs a good food portion.*)

Moje rame je belo. (*My shoulder is white.*)

Hotel „Bor" je dobar hotel. (*Hotel „ Bor " is a good hotel.*)

Borko je dobar tata. (*Borko is a good dad.*)

Kada je rok? (*When is the deadline?*)

3. Write in Latin in your notebook or on a piece of paperand read aloud! – Napiši na latinici i čitaj glasno!

Тамо је мала хала. (*Over there is a small hall.*)

Која је мера? (*What is the measure?*)

Ту је рода. (*Here is a stork.*)

Дара је мала. (*Dara is small.*)

Мато је лекар. (*Mato is a doctor.*)

Та беба је јако лака. (*This baby is very light.*)

Та лутка је добра. (*This doll is good.*)

Вела боја је лепа боја. (*White color is a nice color.*)

То је моје млеко. (*This is my milk.*)

Како је та драга дама? (*How is this nice lady?*)

Ратко је храбар. (*Ratko is brave.*)

Где је лед? (*Where is the ice?*)

Та тема је добра. (*This theme is good.*)

Тај део је добар. (*This part is good.*)

Лола је у клубу. (*Lola is at the club.*)

Моја мама је у граду. (*My mom is in town.*)

Letters: i, n, s, z

Mark letters you already know! – Obeleži slova koja već poznaješ!

A a = А а	Dž dž = Џ џ	I i = И и	N n = Н н	Š š = Ш ш
B b = Б б	Đ đ = Ђ ђ	J j = Ј ј	Nj nj = Њ њ	T t = Т т
C c = Ц ц	E e = Е е	K k = К к	O o = О о	U u = У у
Č č = Ч ч	F f = Ф ф	L l = Л л	P p = П п	V v = В в
Ć ć = Ћ ћ	G g = Г г	Lj lj = Љ љ	R r = Р р	Z z = З з
D d = Д д	H h = Х х	M m = М м	S s = С с	Ž ž = Ж ж

Let's practice the other letters!

Latin script	I	N	S	Z
Cyrillic block letters	**И и**	**Н н**	**С с**	**З з**

1. Write in Cyrillic in your notebook or on a piece of paper and read aloud! – Napiši na ćirilici i čitaj glasno!

idem (*I go*)

keks (*cookie*)

dati (*to give*)

rasti (*to grow*)

barem (*at least*)

Rada

znati (*to know*)

uzeti (*to take*)

stati (*to stop*)

hteti (*to want*)

brati (*to pick*)

ukrasti (*to steal*)

jabuka (*apple*)

orah (*walnut*)

program

hektar (*hectare*)

istorija (*history*)

Zora

meso (*meat*)

izgled (*look*)

hartija (*paper*)

patos (*ground*)

so (*salt*)

med (*honey*)

sos (*sauce*)

zeleno (*green*)

zato (*therefore*)

red (*order*)

zabluda (*error*)

na (*on*)

sa (*with*)

Ines

hijena (*hyena*)

dim (*smoke*)

jela (*fir*)

inat (*definace*)

jagoda (*strawberry*)

Lidija

lek (*medicine*)

gram

niko (*no one*)

jeka (*echo*)

sladoled (*ice cream*)

Radojka

rad (*work*)

sto (*table*)

biber (*pepper*)

riba (*fish*)

dinar

jednak (*same*)

zbog (*because*)

nada (*hope*)

smog

do (*until, up to*)

za (*for*)

tigar

eho (*echo*)

lila (*purple*)

hrast (*oak*)

lud (*crazy*)

2. Write in Cyrillic in your notebook or on a piece of paper and read aloud! – Napiši na ćirilici i čitaj glasno!

Verb TO BE – glagol BITI

ja sam (*I am*)   mi smo (*we are*)

ti si (*you are*)   vi ste (*you are*)

on/ona/ono je (*he/she/it is*)   oni/one/ona su (*they are*)

3. Write in Cyrillic in your notebook or on a piece of paper and read aloud! – Napiši na ćirilici i čitaj glasno!

Numbers – Brojevi

jedan (1), tri (3)

sedam (7), osam (8), deset (10)

jedanaest (11), trinaest (13)

sedamnaest (17), osamnaest (18)

trideset (30), sedamdeset (70), osamdeset (80), sto (100)

4. Write in Cyrillic in your notebook or on a piece of paper and read aloud! – Napiši na ćirilici i čitaj glasno!

Koji je danas dan? (*What day is today?*)

Danas je subota. (*Today is Saturday.*)

Koji je sutra dan? (*What day is tomorrow?*)

Sutra je utorak. (*Tomorrow is Tuesday.*)

Kada idemo da beremo jagode? (*When are we going to pick strawberries?*)

Idemo na izlet? (*Are we going on a trip?*)

Znati ko dolazi – to je dobro. (*Who´s coming – that´s good to know.*)

Mogu da dobijem keks? (*Can I have a cookie?*)

Ona je uzela jaja, meso i ribu. (*She took eggs, meat and.*)

Mogu da ti dam sladoled. (*I can give you an ice cream.*)

U redu? (*All right?*)

Gde stajemo? Kod restorana? (*Where do we stop? At the restaurant?*)

Kako tvoje dete brzo raste! (*How fast is your child growing!*)

Hteli ne hteli, ali mala Radojka je sada velika. (*Whether we want ir or not, but little Radojka is big now.*)

Ah, barem da imaju malo nade! (*Oh, if they had at least a little hope!*)

Molim te, stani! (*Stop, please!*)

Gde rastu tako lepe zelene jabuke? (*Where do such beautiful green apples grow?*)

Mi nismo hteli ni ribu ni sos uz ribu. (*We wanted neither fish nor the sauce with the fish.*)

Ne, mala Rada nije ukrala lila hartiju. (*No, little Rada didn´t steal te purple paper.*)

Ko je tu lud? (*Who is crazy here?*)

Zbog Lidije nisi hteo mleko? (*Because of Lidija you dind´t want milk?*)

Oni su gledali program, a mi nismo. (*They watched the program, but we didn´t.*)

Kada si dao lek Borku? (*When did you give the medicine to Borko?*)

To nije niti jedan gram! (*This is not even a gram!*)

---

5. Write in Latin in your notebook or on a piece of paper and read aloud! – Napiši na latinici i vežbaj čitanje!

Ми добро знамо историју. (*We know very well the history.*)

Нико није тако леп као Лола и Матеј. (*No one is as beautiful as Lola and Matej.*)

Зора је на аеродрому и стоји код таксија. (*Zora is at the airport and stands by the cab station.*)

Јека у хали је једнака као јека у мојој соби. (*The echo in the hall is the same as the one in my room.*)

Ми не једемо месо. (*We don´t eat meat.*)

Ја радо узимам сладолед за десерт. (*I like having an ice cream for dessert.*)

Је ли изглед битан? (*Is the look important?*)

Радојка има велики зелени сто. (*Radojka has a big green table.*)

Рад је лаган ако знамо како да радимо. (*The work is easy if we know how to do it.*)

На патосу је један динар. (*There is one dinar on the floor.*)

И зато не идемо на море? (*And that´s why we don´t go to the sea?*)

Где су со и бибер? (*Where are the salt and papper?*)

Да, морамо да узмемо и мед. (*Yes, we have to take honey too.*)

Ко једе рибу? (*Who eats the fish?*)

Који смог у граду! (*What a smog in the town!*)

Молим кекс уз какао! (*A cookie and the cocoa drink, please !*)

Где су сада тигар и хијена? (*Where are the tiger and hyena now?*)

Реда мора бити! (*There must be order!*)

Ти си у заблуди. (*You are under a mistake.*)

Од Београда до Бора није далеко. (*It´s not far from Belgrade to Bor.*)

Е сад не идем с тобом! (*And now I´m not going with you!*)

Који дуги ехо! (*What a long echo!*)

Ја знам како изгледају храст и јела. (*I know what the oak and the fir look like.*)

Не идемо јер дим је јак. (*We are not going because the smoke is strong.*)

Letters: v, c

Mark letters you already know! – Obeleži slova koja već poznaješ!

A a = A a	Dž dž = Џ џ	I i = И и	N n = Н н	Š š = Ш ш
B b = Б б	Đ đ = Ђ ђ	J j = J j	Nj nj = Њ њ	T t = Т т
C c = Ц ц	E e = E e	K k = К к	O o = O o	U u = У у
Č č = Ч ч	F f = Ф ф	L l = Л л	P p = П п	V v = В в
Ć ć = Ћ ћ	G g = Г г	Lj lj = Љ љ	R r = Р р	Z z = З з
D d = Д д	H h = X x	M m = М м	S s = C c	Ž ž = Ж ж

We will practice other letters:

Latin script	V	C
Cyrillic block letters	**В в**	**Ц ц**

1. Write in Cyrillic in your notebook or on a piece of paper and read aloud! – Napiši na ćirilici i čitaj glasno!

The translation into English can be found at the end of the book under "Key to Exercises"

Supermarket „Tezga"

radno vreme od devet do dvadeset

zatvoreno svaku drugu subotu

Nova roba svaki dan!

Izbor kao u bajci!

Hrana, alkohol, kozmetika i ostale dobre stvari!

Imamo i cigarete i novine!

Vrhunski kvalitet!

Dobre cene!

Devet lokacija u Beogradu!

Blizu tramvajske stanice!

S nama je ugodno!

Mi uvek imamo vremena!

Vidi i uzmi!

2. Write in Cyrillic in your notebook or on a piece of paper and read aloud! – Napiši na ćirilici i čitaj glasno!

The translation into English can be found at the end of the book under "Key to Exercises"

U restoranu

Konobarica: - Dobar dan! Izvolite.

Cveta: - Dobar dan! Imate slobodan sto za dvoje?

Konobarica: - Naravno. Ovde je sto.

Cveta: - Hvala. Imate sladoled? Moj sin voli da jede sladoled.

Konobarica: - Da, imamo sladoled od vanile i jagoda.

Cveta: - Jovice?

Jovica: - Molim sladoled od vanile.

Cveta: - Onda molim jedan sladoled od vanile za mog Jovicu i jedan sladoled od jagoda za mene.

Konobarica: - U redu.

3. Write in Latin in your notebook or on a piece of paper and read aloud! – Napiši na latinici i čitaj glasno!

The translation into English can be found at the end of the book under "Key to Exercises"

Поносни тате

Тата 1: - Моја Вукица воли математику.

Тата 2: - Ах да? То је интересантно. Моја Горица не воли математику, али воли хемију. То је готово исто за мене. Мислим, бројеви су и ту и тамо.

Тата 1: - Не, то није исто. Математика је математика, а хемија је хемија.

Тата 2: - Горица воли не само хемију него и биологију. Згодно, зар не?

Тата 1: - Згодно?

Тата 2: - Да буде лекарка треба хемију и биологију.

4. Write in Latin a in your notebook or on a piece of paper nd read aloud! – Napiši na latinici i čitaj glasno!

The translation into English can be found at the end of the book under "Key to Exercises"

Концерт

Милица: - Идемо на концерт?

Боривоје: - На који концерт?

Милица: - Владо Георгијев има концерт у суботу.

Боривоје: - Стварно?

Милица: - Да.

Боривоје: - То је лепа музика. Ја веома волим такву музику, волим баладе. А карте за концерт?

Милица: - Вук има неколико карата и зове нас да идемо на концерт.

Боривоје: - Супер! Где је концерт?

Милица: - У концертној сали Сава Центра.

Боривоје: - Не знам ту локацију. Ја сам тек од недавно у Београду. Да погледамо на мапи?

Милица: - Не треба. Вук зна где је концертна дворана. А и ја знам.

Боривоје: - Онда назови Вука!

Милица: - Наравно!

Letters: p, š

Mark letters you already know! – Obeleži slova koja već poznaješ!

A a = A a	Dž dž = Џ џ	I i = И и	N n = Н н	Š š = Ш ш
B b = Б б	Đ đ = Ђ ђ	J j = J j	Nj nj = Љ љ	T t = T т
C c = Ц ц	E e = E e	K k = К к	O o = O o	U u = У у
Č č = Ч ч	F f = Ф ф	L l = Л л	P p = П п	V v = В в
Ć ć = Ћ ћ	G g = Г г	Lj lj = Љ љ	R r = P p	Z z = З з
D d = Д д	H h = X x	M m = M м	S s = C c	Ž ž = Ж ж

Now there are more letters:

Latin script	P	Š
Cyrillic block letters	**П п**	**Ш ш**

1. Write in Cyrillic in your notebook or on a piece of paper and read aloud! – Napiši na ćirilici i čitaj glasno!

The translation into English can be found at the end of the book under "Key to Exercises"

Posle odmora

Prodan, Rastko, Siniša i Dušan su opet u Srbiji. Prodan je iz Niša, Rastko je iz Novog Sada, Siniša je iz Kruševca, a Dušan je iz Novog Pazara.

I nekoliko drugarica su ponovo u Srbiji. Čedomirka je iz Subotice, Pavlija je iz Kikinde, Pelagija je iz Despotovca, Podgorka je iz Kragujevca, a Dušica je iz Smedereva.

**2. Write in Cyrillic in your notebook or on a piece of paper and read aloud! –
Napiši na ćirilici i vežbaj čitanje!**

Miloš	Velinka
Uroš	Vera
Borislav	Jelisaveta
Boško	Olivera
Velko	Savka
Veselin	Dubravka
Vidoje	Lepa
Vladan	Svetlana
Vladislav	Spasenija
Gvozden	Pava
David	Pauna
Oliver	Perka
Radivoje	Persa
Raša	Petra
Sava	Gaša
Vojimir	Vujadin
Cvetin	Gavrilo
Jevrem	Spira
Petruška	Jakov
Vukasin	Poleksija

3. Write in Cyrillic in your notebook or on a piece of paper and read aloud! – Napiši na ćirilici i vežbaj čitanje!

Obrenovac	Šabac
Jagodin	Sombor
Loznica	Kostolac
Lazarevac	Vršac
Babušnica	Majdanpek
Sremska Mitrovica	Svilajnac
Leskovac	Crvenka
Aleksandrovac	Bajina Bašta
Velika Plana	Grocka
Dimitrovgrad	Zlatibor
Kladovo	Mladenovac
Negotin	Petrovaradin
Sevojno	Temerin
Umka	Šid

4. Write in Latin in your notebook or on a piece of paper and read aloud! – Napiši na latinici i čitaj glasno!

The translation into English can be found at the end of the book under "Key to Exercises"

Време

Данас је време лепо. Сунце сија и небо је ведро. Наравно, лето је. Али сутра – сутра долази киша. Тако стоји у новинама, у прогнози времена. Ја волим кишу. Киша је топла и угодна. Киша увек охлади врелину. И кад сам на мору, ја волим да пада киша. Киша пада, а ја се купам у мору.

Али киша на мору не пада дуго. И то волим.

5. Write in Latin in your notebook or on a piece of paper and read aloud! – Napiši na latinici i čitaj glasno!

The translation into English can be found at the end of the book under "Key to Exercises"

Договор

Гвозден: - Шта има данас на телевизији?

Светлана: - У пола осам је дневник.

Гвозден: - Знам да је дневник у пола осам. Али шта има после?

Светлана: - После је емисија "Јунаци нашег доба".

Гвозден: - Добро. Има ли нешто друго?

Светлана: - На пример?

Гвозден: - Спорт.

Светлана: - Има. У девет је одбојка… Али на Другом програму је емисија о култури. А ја волим емисије о култури.

Гвозден: - И шта сада да радимо?

Светлана: - Имам идеју. Ако ти опереш судове, гледамо спорт – ако ја оперем судове, гледамо културу.

Гвозден: - …Све судове?

Letters: ž, f, č

Mark letters you already know! – Obeleži slova koja već poznaješ!

A a = А а	Dž dž = Џ џ	I i = И и	N n = Н н	Š š = Ш ш
B b = Б б	Đ đ = Ђ ђ	J j = Ј ј	Nj nj = Њ њ	T t = Т т
C c = Ц ц	E e = Е е	K k = К к	O o = О о	U u = У у
Č č = Ч ч	F f = Ф ф	L l = Л л	P p = П п	V v = В в
Ć ć = Ђ ђ	G g = Г г	Lj lj = Љ љ	R r = Р р	Z z = З з
D d = Д д	H h = Х х	M m = М м	S s = С с	Ž ž = Ж ж

We keep practicing:

Latin script	Ž	F	Č
Cyrillic block letters	**Ж ж**	**Ф ф**	**Ч ч**

1. Write in Cyrillic in your notebook or on a piece of paper and read aloud! – Napiši na ćirilici i čitaj glasno!

The translation into English can be found at the end of the book under "Key to Exercises"

a) Telefoni u Srbiji:

policija – jedan devet dva

vatrogasci – jedan devet tri

tačno vreme – devet pet

brojevi telefona – devet osam osam

vojna policija – devet osam šest nula

b) Govorni automati su:

pravoslavni verski praznici i običaji – devet osam dva dva

meteorološki podaci – devet osam dva tri

loto i sportska prognoza – devet osam četiri četiri

2. Write in Cyrillic in your notebook or on a piece of paper and read aloud! – Napiši na ćirilici i vežbaj čitanje!

The translation into English can be found at the end of the book under "Key to Exercises"

Srpska jela

sarma od kiselog kupusa

paradajz čorba

pogača s blitvom

ajvar od zelenog paradajza

pogača s tikvicama

kolač s muskatnom tikvom

srpska čorba od mesa

junetina s pečurkama

vinski paprikaš od somovine

pržena jaja sa slaninom

zapečena boranija

pastrmka u vinu

belo meso u pavlaci

sarma od slatkog kupusa

kiseli feferoni

biftek

fiš-paprikaš

3. Write in Latin in your notebook or on a piece of paper and read aloud! – Napiši na latinici i čitaj glasno!

The translation into English can be found at the end of the book under "Key to Exercises"

Живан и Јефимија су муж и жена скоро десет година.

Чедомирка и Ружица су сестре и живе у Нишу.

Филипа и Блаженка су другарице и иду на кафу.

Снежана и Божидарка су комшинице и воле фудбал.

Живомир и Надежда су брат и сестра и воле да играју шах.

Желимирка и Момчило иду у биоскоп сваку суботу.

Живка и Чаславка студирају филозофију.

Филотеј и Софија иду у основну школу.

Божана и Живана су професорке на универзитету.

4. Write in Latin in your notebook or on a piece of paper and read aloud! – Napiši na latinici i čitaj glasno!

The translation into English can be found at the end of the book under "Key to Exercises"

У Србији можете да посетите фантастичне локале и ресторане, добре пабове и локале с модерном музиком као и традиционалне кафане. Читав дан можете да купујете у веома интересантним и добрим местима за шопинг. Желите да видите знаменитости Србије? Можете да посетите манастире и цркве – они су важни део српске културе и традиције. Исто тако можете да одете у музеје и галерије у свим градовима. У градовима можете да уживате у баровима, можете да откријете чари београдских сплавова и да посетите чаробне клубове. Ако желите да научите српски језик, можете да упишете течај српског језика. Ако тражите ексклузивни градски хотел или желите да одседнете у етно селу, и у томе можете да уживате у Србији.

5. Read aloud! – Čitaj glasno!

The translation into English can be found at the end of the book under "Key to Exercises"

форум, футур, чај, фокус, чембало, фарса, анемичан, флаша, антипатичан, форма, Жаклина, физика, Фигаро, Ружа, факат, артичока, чили, фосил, Фанија, фуснота, фигура, Филипа, фолија, фактор, Живадинка, фешта, палачинка, фузија, фунта, Живанка, фијакер, форте, фамилија, жирафа, фамозан, практичан, фанатик, жири, фарма, феномен, дефинитивно, фармер, фасциниран, делфин, фаталан, флора, фауна, филозофија, федерација, фестивал, фолклор, фигуративан, тајфун, филм Живослава, филтер, финалист, тарифа, финиш, фирма, тријумф, формулар, Живкица, функција, биографија

Letters: ć, nj, lj

Mark letters you already know! – Obeleži slova koja već poznaješ!

A a = A a	Dž dž = Џ џ	I i = И и	N n = Н н	Š š = Ш ш
B b = Б б	Đ đ = Ђ ђ	J j = J j	Nj nj = Њ њ	T t = T т
C c = Ц ц	E e = E e	K k = K к	O o = O o	U u = У у
Č č = Ч ч	F f = Ф ф	L l = Л л	P p = П п	V v = B в
Ć ć = Ћ ћ	G g = Г г	Lj lj = Љ љ	R r = P p	Z z = З з
D d = Д д	H h = X x	M m = M м	S s = C c	Ž ž = Ж ж

We keep practicing:

Latin script	Ć	Nj	Lj
Cyrillic block letters	**Ћ ћ**	**Њ њ**	**Љ љ**

1. Write in Cyrillic in your notebook or on a piece of paper and read aloud! – Napiši na ćirilici i čitaj glasno!

The translation into English can be found at the end of the book under "Key to Exercises"

jagnjetina s pasuljem

srpske ćufte

pljeskavica na srpski način

riblja čorba

svinjski ražnjići sa žalfijom

pirinač s povrćem

proja sa spanaćem

žuti pasulj s govedinom

teleća kisela čorba

keleraba sa ćuftama

paprike punjene lignjama

svinjetina u sosu od ajvara

ražnjići od piletine sa sosom od oraha

kisele paprike punjene sirom

pasulj na starinski način

mešani pileći ražnjići

2. Write in Cyrillic in your notebook or on a piece of paper and read aloud! – Napiši na ćirilici i čitaj glasno!

The translation into English can be found at the end of the book under "Key to Exercises"

Detinjstvo

Ja se dobro sećam mojih školskih drugova i drugarica. Moj najbolji drug se zvao Ljubomir Presanović. On je sedeo sa mnom u klupi i svi su ga zvali Ljuba. Ja sam uvek igrao s njim i sa Smiljanom fudbal na velikom odmoru. Da je Smiljana igrala s nama fudbal, nije bilo neobično: kad smo deca, onda nema razlike – svi se igramo zajedno. Smilja je bila zaljubljena u Dragoljuba. Njega smo zvali Dragan i on je bio najbolji učenik u razredu. On je sedeo sa Željkom u klupi i oni su bili zaljubljeni. Mnogo devojčica u razredu su bile zaljubljene u Dragana. Posebno Bosiljka, Milja i Dunja. U Bosiljku, Milju i Dunju su bili drugi dečaci zaljubljeni: u Bosiljku je bio zaljubljen Ljuba, u Milju je bio zaljubljen Ognjen, a u Dunju je bio zaljubljen Nemanja. Kad je u razred došao Uglješa Perić, onda se sve promenilo. I ljubav, i drugarstvo i fudbal. Zapravo ne znam da li se sve promenilo zbog Uglješe Perića

3. Write in Latin in your notebook or on a piece of paper and read aloud! – Napiši na latinici i čitaj glasno!

The translation into English can be found at the end of the book under "Key to Exercises"

Радња мојег оца

Ја се зовем Ћанка Дражић и живим у Дорћолу. Дорћол се налази у центру Београда. Моји родитељи имају малу стару кућу где сам ја одрасла. Наша кућа има приземље, први и други спрат. Ми живимо на првом и другом спрату, а у приземљу куће мој отац има радњу. Он је кројач у трећој генерацији. Он углавном ради оправке одеће за своје сталне муштерије. Чак и недељом. Иако он не може да пуно заради и иако има велику конкуренцију у скупим радњама, он воли свој посао.

4. Write in Latin in your notebook or on a piece of paper and read aloud! – Napiši na latinici i čitaj glasno!

The translation into English can be found at the end of the book under "Key to Exercises"

Бање у Србији

У Србији су бање веома омиљене. Врњачка Бања је веома лепа бања и има чак седам извора лековите воде. Сокобања је исто тако лепа бања и њене воде су добре против астме и дисајних проблема. Бања Ковиљача или Краљевска бања има богату историју и дугу традицију у лечењу остеопорозе и реуме. Нишка Бања је једна од најпопуларнијих бања у Србији и њени лекарски тимови су одлични у дијагностици. Овчар Бања је у центру нетакнуте природе и њена вода има тридесет осам степена. Бања Кањижа се налази у Војводини и њене воде су невероватно топле – између педесет и седамдесет степена.

Letters: dž, đ

Mark letters you already know! – Obeleži slova koja već poznaješ!

A a = А а	Dž dž = Џ џ	I i = И и	N n = Н н	Š š = Ш ш
B b = Б б	Đ đ = Ђ ђ	J j = Ј ј	Nj nj = Њ њ	T t = Т т
C c = Ц ц	E e = Е е	K k = К к	O o = О о	U u = У у
Č č = Ч ч	F f = Ф ф	L l = Л л	P p = П п	V v = В в
Ć ć = Ћ ћ	G g = Г г	Lj lj = Љ љ	R r = Р р	Z z = З з
D d = Д д	H h = Х х	M m = М м	S s = С с	Ž ž = Ж ж

We keep practicing:

Latin script	Dž	Đ
Cyrillic block letters	**Џ џ**	**Ђ ђ**

1. Write in Cyrillic in your notebook or on a piece of paper and read aloud! – Napiši na ćirilici i vežbaj čitanje!

The translation into English can be found at the end of the book under "Key to Exercises"

Koja jela volimo?

Ja volim đuveč. Moja mama voli pileću džigericu. Moj tata voli leđnu slaninu. Moja starija sestra Rađa voli kolače sa smeđim šećerom. Moj mlađi brat Đorđe voli grožđe i kolače koji se zovu medveđe šape. Moja tetka Anđelka voli čorbu od medveđeg luka. Moja strina Đurđa voli sok od đumbira. Moj

---

stric Đuro voli sva jela s patlidžanom. Moja baba Anđa voli džem od šljiva i džem od kajsija.

2. Write in Cyrillic in your notebook or on a piece of paper and read aloud! – Napiši na ćirilici i vežbaj čitanje!

The translation into English can be found at the end of the book under "Key to Exercises"

Moja sestra

Moja sestra se zove Đulijana i ja je jako volim. Ali ono što ja ne volim kod nje jeste njeno traženje stvari po kući. U subotu je, na primer, ceo dan tražila svoje smeđe đinđuve. Na kraju ih je našla, ali i ja sam morao da tražim te đinđuve. Ali – moram da priznam – i ona meni pomaže kod domaćih zadataka pa je fer da i ja njoj ponekad pomažem. Ali prekjuče je opet bila potraga za njenim stvarima – za pidžamom. Ona je rekla: „Đurice, budi džentlmen i pomozi dami u nevolji." Tako sam i ja tražio pidžamu. I našli smo pidžamu u džaku za staru odeću. Kako je ona tamo došla, ja to ne znam. Sada tražimo njen džemper i čizme. Đulijana je rekla da ću da dobijem pola njenog džeparca ako ih nađem.

3. Write in Latin in your notebook or on a piece of paper and read aloud! – Napiši na latinici i vežbaj čitanje!

The translation into English can be found at the end of the book under "Key to Exercises"

Оглас

Издајемо мали намештени двособни стан у Београду са централним грејањем. Стан је нов и у близини је аутобуска станица и пијаца. У кварту се налази такође и енглески колеџ Џорџ Бајрон као и основна школа. Стан изнајмљујемо и породицама и студентима.

4. Write in Latin in your notebook or on a piece of paper and read aloud! – Napiši na latinici i vežbaj čitanje!

The translation into English can be found at the end of the book under "Key to Exercises"

Ћевабџиница "Весели ћевапи"

У улици Џорџа Вашингтона отворена је ћевабџиница "Весели ћевапи". Власник ћевабџинице је инжењер Ђуро Ђорђевић и госпођа Ђурђица Самарџић. Нова ћевабџиница има на понуди класичне ћевапе и локал је веома угодан. Кад смо питали зашто се њихова радња зове „Весели ћевапи", господин Ђорђевић је рекао: "Кад видим десет малих ћевапа на тањиру, онда они изгледају за мене као мала весела деца. Зато се наша радња зове "Весели ћевапи".

5. Write in Latin in your notebook or on a piece of paperand read aloud! – Napiši na latinici i vežbaj čitanje!

The translation into English can be found at the end of the book under "Key to Exercises"

Телефонски бројеви

Хитна помоћ – један девет четири

Војна хитна помоћ – девет седам шест

Пријава телефонских сметњи – девет седам седам

Помоћ на путу – девет осам седам

Служба буђења – девет осам један један

Разна обавештења – девет осам један два

Block Letters in Cursive – *štampana kosa slova*

	A	B	C	Č	Ć
Block letters	А а	Б б	Ц ц	Ч ч	Ћ ћ
Block letters in cursive	*А а*	*Б б*	*Ц ц*	*Ч ч*	*Ћ ћ*

	D	Dž	Đ	E	F
Block letters	Д д	Џ џ	Ђ ђ	Е е	Ф ф
Block letters in cursive	*Д g*	*Џ џ*	*Ђ ђ*	*Е е*	*Ф ф*

	G	H	I	J	K
Block letters	Г г	Х х	И и	Ј ј	К к
Block letters in cursive	*Г ī*	*Х х*	*И и*	*Ј ј*	*К к*

	L	Lj	M	N	Nj
Block letters	Л л	Љ љ	М м	Н н	Њ њ
Block letters in cursive	*Л л*	*Љ љ*	*М м*	*Н н*	*Њ њ*

	O	P	R	S	Š
Block letters	О о	П п	Р р	С с	Ш ш
Block letters in cursive	*О о*	*П ū*	*Р р*	*С с*	*Ш ш*

	T	U	V	Z	Ž
Block letters	Т т	У у	В в	З з	Ж ж
Block letters in cursive	*Т ū̄*	*У у*	*В в*	*З з*	*Ж ж*

You´ve noticed: the letters in cursive are almost the same as block letters. Except for five letters: **D, G, I, P** and **T** and only as **lowercase letters**.

	D	G	I	P	T
Block letters	Д д	Г г	И и	П п	Т т
Block letters in cursive	*Д g*	*Г ī*	*И и*	*П ū*	*Т ū̄*

Block **letters in cursive** are used in printed materials - books, newspapers, etc. - and are **for reading, not writing**. Therefore, in this lesson there are **only reading exercises**. For writing, one uses the Cyrillic writing script, which will be introduced in the next lesson.

Let's have a look at the first three letters:

	D	G	I
Block letters	Д д	Г г	И и
Block letters in cursive	*Д д*	*Г г*	*И и*

1. Read aloud! – Vežbaj čitanje!

дефинитивно	*дискета*	*птицама*
кандидат	*цигарета*	*адмирал*
папагај	*парадајз*	*катедрала*
граматика	*дигресија*	*дијамант*
метеорологија	*вага*	*дресура*
археологија	*диносаурус*	*кондор*
фудбал	*бас*	*бифе*
шофер	*дискусија*	*Балкан*
кафа	*џем*	*лорд*
беџ	*магазин*	*рум*
сноб	*филм*	*џунгла*
гроф	*кугла*	*шминка*
шунка	*хокеј*	*ас*
бригада	*водвиљ*	*бал*
биро	*гаранција*	*дама*
гардероба	*дренажа*	*командир*
курир	*манир*	*мода*
модел	*резерва*	*арија*
милион	*каса*	*лава*
салама	*фреска*	*гама*

Let's have a look at the remaining two letters:

	Р	Т
Block letters	П п	Т т
Block letters in cursive	*П п̄*	*Т т̄*

2. Read aloud! – Vežbaj čitanje!

хоризонт	*фанатичан*	*кактус*
палма	*ћевапчићи*	*степа*
антилопа	*бисквит*	*султан*
евентуално	*апостол*	*Торонто*
антипатичан	*Тимотије*	*пол*
Тара	*старт*	*еквадор*
наутика	*банка*	*Павле*
фантазија	*комет*	*спорт*
планет	*тулипан*	*парола*
зенит	*телевизија*	*Тихана*
Томо	*астрономија*	*тата*
Јупитер	*албатрос*	*центар*
Венера	*олтар*	*патрола*
хеликоптер	*марципан*	*паб*
историја	*атом*	*папир*
бестселер	*териториј*	*Ниш*
вакуум	*хијена*	*Сатурн*
трамвај	*метеорит*	*зебра*
стоп	*екран*	*Марс*
Сибир	*арсенал*	*комисија*
барака	*фризура*	*кафана*
кукуруз	*киви*	*балет*

биоīрафија	*мајор*	*радио*
реализација	*ракија*	*сардина*
Барселона	*арūикл*	*козмонауū*
Маđарска	*банкеū*	*Неūūун*
виолина	*конūрабас*	*клавир*
дириīенū	*йолиција*	*ауūо*
Адам	*Сокраū*	*инūервју*
дуеū	*комйјуūер*	*ūелефон*
конфликū	*инūернационалан*	*йудинī*
џемйер	*кромйир*	*мајсūор*
фуūрола	*арūиљерија*	*армија*
Букуреūū	*канūон*	*йараф*
айоūека	*комйас*	*салаūа*
сируй	*воūка*	*меūал*

3. Read aloud! – Vežbaj čitanje!

The translation into English can be found at the end of the book under "Key to Exercises"

<u>*Оīласи*</u>

Удовац *(45 īодина) из Беоīрада, йо занимању механичар, ūражи йарūнерку. Хобији: ауūомобили, фудбал и шеūње уз Дунав. Волим да кувам и да се бринем о кући. Жеље: брак и деца. Шифра: "Заувек ūвој"*

Удовица *(35 īодина) из Ниша, йо занимању медицинска сесūра, ūражи йарūнера. Немам децу, волим да йишем йоезију. Иако йишем йоезију, нисам романūична: не волим да шеūам и да īледам звезде йо ноћи. Волим да иīрам одбојку и да излазим. Шифра: "Живоū је краūак"*

---

4. Read aloud! – Vežbaj čitanje!

The translation into English can be found at the end of the book under "Key to Exercises"

Перфекшни дан

Данас имам слободан дан. То је лейо. Не морам нишша да радим. Значи: мойу да радим шша хоћу. Данас мойу да йијем кафу на миру, мойу да доручкујем дуйо, мойу да идем у йрад. Шша мойу да радим у йраду? Мойу да йосешим Марију. Да, мойу да одем до ње и да је йишам како је. Онда можемо да идемо заједно на ручак. Где не ручак? Да, шо је добро йишање. Али Марија сийурно зна добре ресшоране. После ручка можемо да одемо у йарк, да седимо на клуйи и да йричамо. То је лейо – йарк у йролеће. Увече можемо да идемо у биоской или у йозоришше. У биоскойима има увек добрих филмова и у йозоришшу има увек добрих йредсшава. После можемо да одемо у неки ноћни клуб и да ийрамо. Или само да слушамо музику. То је лейо. Имаши йерфекшни дан.

5. Read aloud! – Vežbaj čitanje!

The translation into English can be found at the end of the book under "Key to Exercises"

Цишаши

Мој син се зове Тимошије и има йеш йодина. Он има веома занимљиве мисли и ја морам да йа циширам. Он каже на йример:

> *Данас нема сунца јер се сунце још није йробудило.*

> *Моја бака је дебела јер она носи йуно речи у себи.*

> *Ја волим да идем у золошки врш јер шамо мойу да видим мајмуне који се смеју људима.*

> *Мој шаша йонекад комйликује моју маму, а моја мама йонекад не разуме шша мој шаша йовори.*

> *Ја волим да идем на село код бабе Даре јер она има кокошке које су йриродне.*

6. Read aloud! – Vežbaj čitanje!

The translation into English can be found at the end of the book under "Key to Exercises"

Поруке

На столу лежи порука од Петра:

Долазим за йеш минуша. Зашшо не ради швој мобилни шелефон?

Након десет минута Гордана чита поруку и пише поруку:

Ја идем код фризера. Долазим за шри саша. Не знам зашшо не ради мој мобилни.

Након три сата Петар пише поруку:

Где си? Не јављаш се на мобилни. Ја сада идем код механичара. Долазим за двадесеш минуша.

Након тридесет минута Гордана пише поруку:

Зашшо сада не ради швој мобилни? Када долазиш? Ја морам да идем у школу збоī Драīана, данас је родишељски сасшанак. Долазимо кући йосле йеш.

У шест Петар пише поруку:

Где сше? Ја не волим да йишем йоруке на харшији ако већ сви имамо мобилне. Идем на шренинī. Долазим око осам.

У девет Гордана пише поруку:

Где си? Вечера је на сшолу, ја сйавам. Сушра сам цео дан на конференцији. А ши?

Cyrillic Written Letters – *ćirilična pisana slova*

		A	B	C	Č	Ć
Block letters		А а	Б б	Ц ц	Ч ч	Ћ ћ
Block letters in cursive		*А а*	*Б б*	*Ц ц*	*Ч ч*	*Ћ ћ*
Written letters		*А а*	*Б б*	*Ц ц*	*Ч ч*	*Ћ ћ*

		D	Dž	Đ	E	F
Block letters		Д д	Џ џ	Ђ ђ	Е е	Ф ф
Block letters in cursive		*Д д*	*Џ џ*	*Ђ ђ*	*Е е*	*Ф ф*
Written letters		*Д д*	*Џ џ*	*Ђ ђ*	*Е е*	*Ф ф*

		G	H	I	J	K
Block letters		Г г	Х х	И и	Ј ј	К к
Block letters in cursive		*Г г*	*Х х*	*И и*	*Ј ј*	*К к*
Written letters		*Г г*	*Х х*	*И и*	*Ј ј*	*К к*

		L	Lj	M	N	Nj
Block letters		Л л	Љ љ	М м	Н н	Њ њ
Block letters in cursive		*Л л*	*Љ љ*	*М м*	*Н н*	*Њ њ*
Written letters		*Л л*	*Љ љ*	*М м*	*Н н*	*Њ њ*

		O	P	R	S	Š
Block letters		О о	П п	Р р	С с	Ш ш
Block letters in cursive		*О о*	*П п*	*Р р*	*С с*	*Ш ш*
Written letters		*О о*	*П п*	*Р р*	*С с*	*Ш ш*

	T	U	V	Z	Ž
Block letters	Т т	У у	В в	З з	Ж ж
Block letters in cursive	*Т т*	*У у*	*В в*	*З з*	*Ж ж*
Written letters	*Т т*	*У у*	*В в*	*З з*	*Ж ж*

The written script – *pisana slova* is used only for **writing**. All typed documents are logically written with block letters or block letters in cursive. But on the other hand, the handwritten texts are also read - that's why more **writing and reading exercises** follow.

You have already noticed the similarity with block letters and with block letters in cursive. There are some other differences and they are in six letters: **D, G, I, P, Š** and **T**.

	D	G	I	P	Š	T
Block letters	Д д	Г г	И и	П п	Ш ш	Т т
Block letters in cursive	*Д д*	*Г г*	*И и*	*П n*	*Ш ш*	*Т m*
Written letters	*Д g*	*Г i*	*И u*	*П ü*	*Ш ш*	*Т т*

1. Write all the written letters in your notebook or on a piece of paper! – Prepiši sva pisana slova!

Let's practice the first three written letters:

	D	G	I
Block letters	Д д	Г г	И и
Written letters	*Д g*	*Г i*	*И u*

2. Write in written letters in your notebook or on a piece of paper and read aloud! – Napiši na pisanoj ćirilici i vežbaj čitanje!

galaksija = *галаксија*	muzika
agava	smog
ada	majka
akacija	Sava
Indija	ekologija
geografija	alkohol
menza	huligan
bambus	Ilija
vikend	soda
banda	jubilej
deo	civilizacija
hiljada	masovno
agrar	ajvar
aukcija	bilans
decidiran	digresija
dresura	imigracija
kadifa	konfuzija
konkavan	musaka
oralan	rival
vezir	Danska

3. Write in written letters in your notebook or on a piece of paper and read aloud! – Napiši na pisanoj ćirilici i vežbaj čitanje!

Draga Gordana!	Dragi Njegoslave!
Draga Dunja!	Dragi Dragoljube!
Draga Smiljana!	Dragi Ljubo!

	P	Š	T
Block letters	П п	Ш ш	Т т
Written letters	*П п*	*Ш ш*	*Т т*

4. Write in written letters in your notebook or on a piece of paper and read aloud! – Napiši na pisanoj ćirilici i vežbaj čitanje!

afinitet = *афинитет*

afinitet = *афинитет*	amortizer
bagatela	desert
citadela	plasman
duplikat	emigrant
entitet	evidentno
fundament	gabarit
insekt	integritet
intencija	intenzitet
irelevantan	notoran
kontradiktoran	opsesija
orbita	plafon
proces	pumpa
pompa	relevantan
rabat	spontano
striktan	šansona
šank	tendencija
terakota	tirada
trik	vijadukt
vinjeta	šarlatan
kompot	viski

5. Write in written letters in your notebook or on a piece of paper and read aloud! – Napiši na pisanoj ćirilici i vežbaj čitanje!

Poštovani gospodine Markoviću!

Poštovana gospođo Perić!

Poštovani gospodine Vladiću!

Poštovana gospođo Jovanović!

6. Write the text in your notebook or on a piece of paper and read it loud! – Prepiši tekst i vežbaj čitanje!

The translation into English can be found at the end of the book under "Key to Exercises"

Месеци у години су: јануар, фебруар, март, април, мај, јуни, јули, август, септембар, октобар, новембар и децембар.

Дани у недељи су: понедељак, уторак, среда, четвртак, петак, субота и недеља.

Годишња доба су: пролеће, лето, јесен и зима.

7. Write the text in your notebook or on a piece of paper in written letters! – Prepiši tekst ćiriličnim pisanim slovima!

The translation into English can be found at the end of the book under "Key to Exercises"

Novi film

Danilo: - Idemo danas u bioskop?

Mila: - Dobra ideja. Šta gledamo?

Danilo: - Znaš film „Bilo jednom u Srbiji"?

Mila: - Ne, ne znam. To je novi film?

Danilo: - Da.

Mila: - Je li to drama?

Danilo: - I drama i komedija. Kritičari kažu da je to dobar film. Igraju dobri glumci i glumice.

Mila: - Može. Ja volim da gledam domaće filmove.

Answer the questions and write in written script in your notebook or on a piece of paper! – Odgovori pismeno koristeći ćirilična pisana slova! 

1. Ko ide u bioskop?

2. Koji je film u bioskopu?

3. Je li to novi film?

4. Je li film drama ili komedija?

5. Šta kažu kritičari za film?

6. Ko igra u filmu?

7. Da li Mila voli da gleda domaće filmove?

8. Read and answer the questions in your notebook or on a piece of paper! – Čitaj i odgovori na pitanja! 

The translation into English can be found at the end of the book under "Key to Exercises"

Идемо у позориште

Смиљана: - Хоћемо у позориште?

Вук: - Наравно. То желимо већ дуго. Шта има на репертоару?

Смиљана: - "Госпођа министарка" игра у Народном позоришту.

Вук: - Одлично. Ја волим Бранислава Нушића. Он је мој омиљени писац.

Смиљана: - И мој.

Вук: - Кад су представе?

Смиљана: - У суботу је премијера.

Вук: - Онда идемо у суботу.

Питања:

1. Да ли Смиљана и Вук желе већ дуго да иду у позориште?

2. Што има на репертоару у Народном позоришту?

---

3. Ко воли Бранислава Нушића?

4. Када је премијера?

5. Да ли Смиљана и Вук иду на премијеру?

9. Read and answer the questions in your notebook or on a piece of paper! – Čitaj i odgovori na pitanja!

The translation into English can be found at the end of the book under "Key to Exercises"

<u>Како изгледа моја учитељица?</u>

Моја учитељица се зове Звездана и она је млада. Она има дугу смеђу косу и плаве очи. Она је висока и витка. Моја учитељица често носи кошуље и панталоне. Понекад носи сукњу. Моја учитељица се често смеје и зато ја волим моју учитељицу.

Питања:

1. Како се зове његова учитељица?

2. Је ли она стара?

3. Какву косу има Звездана?

4. Какве су њене очи?

5. Је ли она ниска?

6. Је ли она витка или пунашна?

7. Шта често носи Звездана?

8. Шта понекад носи Звездана?

9. Зашто он воли учитељицу Звездану?

10. Write the text in Latin in your notebook or on a piece of paper and read it loud! – Prepiši tekst na latinicu i čitaj glasno!

The translation into English can be found at the end of the book under "Key to Exercises"

Знам ћирилицу!

Шта сада могу? Сада могу да читам књиге, новине и на интернету различите сајтове. Могу да пишем мејлове и смс-ове. Могу да читам називе улица и називе продавница без проблема. Могу чак да пишем мој приватни дневник на ћирилици. Могу да напишем књигу на ћирилици. То је интересантно јер ја већ дуго скупљам идеје за моју књигу. Али не желим одмах да пишем на ћирилици него тек после.

Ово су моје идеје:

- *Мој јунак се зове Лукас. Он је професор географије и воли да путује. Као ја.*

- *Он жели да посети Србију јер тамо има родбину. Зашто? Његова мама је из Србије.*

- *Шта је његов проблем? Он не зна српски и не зна ћирилицу. То није велики проблем јер родбина зна енглески. Његов проблем је што он жели да иде сваке године у Србију. Дакле, он треба Српски и ћирилицу.*

- *Он жели да упозна Београд, Нови Сад и Ниш.*

То је све од идеја. Засада.

Ах, да! Ово је идеја од данас, записао сам је на цедуљи:

- Мој Лукас треба да упозна девојку. Она се зове Соња. Она исто воли да путује као Лукас. Али она жели да упозна Европу. То је проблем за Лукаса. Шта Лукас може да направи? Може да путује са Соњом по Европи или да остане у Србији.

Да, то су моје идеје. Али те идеје већ могу да пишем и на латиници и на ћирилици.

11. Write the whole „azbuka" in Cyrillic in your notebook or on a piece of paper: block letters, block letters in cursive and written letters! – Napiši azbuku na ćirilici: štampana slova, štampana kosa slova i pisana slova!

AZBUKA

	A	B	V	G	D
Block letters					
Block letters in cursive					
Written letters					

	Đ	E	Ž	Z	I
Block letters					
Block letters in cursive					
Written letters					

	J	K	L	Lj	M
Block letters					
Block letters in cursive					
Written letters					

	N	Nj	O	P	R
Block letters					
Block letters in cursive					
Written letters					

	S	T	Ć	U	F
Block letters					
Block letters in cursive					
Written letters					

	H	C	Č	Dž	Š
Block letters					
Block letters in cursive					
Written letters					

The fonts for Cyrillic used in this book are:

(a) for block letters: Times New Roman – size 12

b) for block letters in cursive: Adamant BG Italic – size 10.5

c) for written letters: Lovely Sofia BG – size 16

2. lekcija

1. Write in Cyrillic in your notebook or on a piece of paper and read aloud! – Napiši na ćirilici i čitaj glasno!

mama (*mom*) = **мама**

tata (*dad*) = **тата**

jako (*very*) = **јако**

tamo (*there, over there*) = **тамо**

ako (*when, if*) = **ако**

tek (*first, just*) = **тек**

koji (*which - male*) = **који**

kome (*whom*) = **коме**

je (*is*) = **је**

meta (*target*) = **мета**

kej (*kai*) = **кеј**

motka (*rod, bar*) = **мотка**

jato (*swarm*) = **јато**

jama (*pit*) = **јама**

tako (*so*) = **тако**

kako (*how*) = **како**

jaje (*egg*) = **јаје**

ja (*I*) = **ја**

ko (*who*) = **ко**

moj (*my*) = **мој**

koja (*which - female*) = **која**

jeka (*echo*) = **јека**

moja (*my - female*) = **моја**

tama (*darkness*) = **тама**

kajak (*kayak*) = **кајак**

mek (*soft*) = **мек**

tok (*run, course*) = **ток**

mak (*poppy*) = **мак**

2. Write in Cyrillic in your notebook or on a piece of paper and read aloud! – Napiši na ćirilici i čitaj glasno!

mom = **мама**

How? = **Како?**

very = **јако**

I = **ја**

my (*male*) = **мој**

Which (*male*)? = **Који?**

Whom? = **Коме?**

dad = **тата**

So. = **Тако.**

there = **тамо**

Who? = **Ко?**

kai = **кеј**

Which (*female*)? = **Која?**

when, if = **ако**

first, just = **тек**   egg = **jaje**

3. Write in Cyrillic in your notebook or on a piece of paper and read aloud! – Napiši na ćirilici i čitaj glasno!

Personal names:

Tomo = **Томо**   Momo = **Момо**

Mato = **Мато**   Tom = **Том**

Kata = **Ката**   Matej = **Матеj**

Maja = **Маja**   Kaja = **Каja**

4. Write in Cyrillic in your notebook or on a piece of paper and read aloud! – Napiši na ćirilici i čitaj glasno!

Kaja je mama. (*Kaja is a mom.*) = **Каja je мама.**

Ko je tata? (*Who is a dad?*) = **Ко je тата?**

Tomo je tata. (*Tomo is a dad.*) = **Томо je тата.**

Kako je Maja? (*How is Maja?*) = **Како je Маja?**

Ko je Momo? (*Who is Momo?*) = **Ко je Момо?**

Moj kajak je mek. (*My kayak is soft.*) = **Моj каjак je мек.**

Moja Kata je tamo. (*My Kata is over there.*) = **Моja Ката je тамо.**

Koja Maja? (*Which Maja?*) = **Коja Маja?**

3. lekcija

1. Write in Cyrillic in your notebook or on a piece of paper and read aloud! – Napiši na ćirilici i čitaj glasno!

komet (*comet*) = **комет**   koga (*who - acc.*) = **кога**

gde (*where*) = где   taj (*this*) = таj

Beograd = Београд   deda (*grandpa*) = деда

tada (*then*) = тада   more (*sea*) = море

draga (*dear - feminine*) = драга   beba (*baby*) = беба

dama (*lady*) = дама   kada (*when*) = када

---

drama = драма

grad (*town*) = град

kome (*whom*) = коме

metar = метар

boem (*bohemian*) = боем

toga (*this - acc.masuline*) = тога

boja (*color*) = боја

gaj (*grove*) = гај

magma = магма

jod (*iodine*) = јод

gora (*mountain*) = гора

geg (*gag)* = гег

Tara = Тара

bor (*fir tree*) = бор

tera = тера

domet (*range*) = домет

deo (*part*) = део

jad (*misery*) = јад

tome (*to this - dat. masuline*) = томе

rado (*gladly*) = радо

bager (*digger*) = багер

ideja (*idea*) = идеја

treba (*needs*) = треба

kratak (*short - masculine*) = кратак

baba (*grandma*) = баба

aerodrom (*airport*) = аеродром

dobar (*good*) = добар

ker (*dog*) = кер

Kaja = Каја

dok (*while*) = док

obrok (*portion*) = оброк

Mara = Мара

Bog (*God*) = Бог

doba (*season*) = доба

beta = бета

Dara = Дара

tema (*theme*) = тема

rok (*deadline*) = рок

mrak (*darkness*) = мрак

grm (*gush*) = грм

batak (*chicken leg*) = батак

kratka (*short – feminine*) = кратка

Magda = Магда

to (*this*) = то

2. Write in Latin in your notebook or on a piece of paper and read aloud! – Napiši na latinici i čitaj glasno!

мама, тата, баба, деда (*mom, dad, grandma, grandpa*) = mama, tata, baba, deda

мој аеродром (*my airport*) = moj aerodrom

моја тема (*my theme*) = moja tema

моја беба (*my baby*) = moja beba

кратка драма (*a short drama*) = kratka drama

То је мој оброк. (*This is my food portion.*) = To je moj obrok.

Дара треба море. (*Dara needs the sea.*) = Dara treba more.

Београд је мој град. (*Belgrade is my city.*) = Beograd je moj grad.

Како је мама? (*How´s mom?*) = Kako je mama?

Како је тата? (*How´s dad?*) = Kako je tata?

Где је Мара? (*Where´s Mara?*) = Gde je Mara?

3. Write in Cyrillic in your notebook or on a piece of paper and translate! – Napiši na ćirilici i prevedi!

Draga! Kako si? = Драга! Како си? = My dear! How are you?

Ja sam dobro. = Ја сам добро. = I am fine.

Kako je beba? = Како је беба? = How is the baby?

Gde je moj tata? = Где је мој тата? = Where is my dad?

To je dobra ideja. = То је добра идеја. = That‘s a good idea.

Gde je more? = Где је море? = Where is the sea?

Tamo je more. = Тамо је море. = Over there is the sea.

Gde je Mara? = Где је Мара? = Where is Mara?

Ko to treba? = Ко то треба? = Who needs it?

Ja to trebam. = Ја то требам. = I need this.

4. lekcija

1. Write in Cyrillic in your notebook or on a piece of paper and read aloud! – Napiši na ćirilici i čitaj glasno!

hotel (*hotel*) = хотел

mleko (*milk*) = млеко

tu (*here*) = ту

luk (*onion*) = лук

hrabar (*brave*) = храбар

rame (*shoulder*) = раме

guma (*rubber*) = гума

let (*flight*) = лет

lekar (*doctor*) = лекар

kuda (*where to*) = куда

led (*ice*) = лед

Ratko = Ратко

lakat (*elbow*) = лакат

beo (*white*) = бео

rum (*rum*) = рум

hala (*hall*) =   хала

duga (*rainbow*) = дуга

dur (*major - music*) = дур

klub (*club*) = клуб

lama (*llama*) = лама

lutka (*doll*) = лутка

buka (*noise)* = бука

Goga = Гога

rub (*edge*) = руб

bubamara (*ladybug*) = бубамара

duh (*spirit*) = дух

rat (war) = рат

mera (*measure*) = мера

u (*in*) = у

kula (*tower*) = кула

mol (*minor - music*) = мол

Lela = Лела

hram (*temple*) = храм

Homer = Хомер

lom (*break*) = лом

hod (*walk*) = ход

roda (*stork*) = рода

lug (*floodplain forest*) = луг

lira (*lyre*) = лира

letak (*pamphlet*) = летак

2. Write in Cyrillic in your notebook or on a piece of paper and read aloud! – Napiši na ćirilici i čitaj glasno!

Lara je moja beba. (*Lara is my baby.*) = Лара је моја беба.

To je jako dobar hotel. (*This is a very good hotel.*) = То је јако добар хотел.

Tu je bela kula. (*Here is the white tower.*) = Ту је бела кула.

Moj lakat je kratak. (*My elbow is short.*) = Мој лакат је кратак.

Mleko je belo. (*Milk is white.*) = Млеко је бело.

Boba je mala. (*Boba is small.*) = Боба је мала.

Moj lekar je dobar. (*My doctor is good.*) = Мој лекар је добар.

Moj tata je hrabar. (*My dad is brave.*) = Мој тата је храбар.

Moja lutka je meka. (*My doll is soft.*) = Моја лутка је мека.

Ko je ta dama? (*Who is this lady?*) = Ко је та дама?

Gde je luk? (*Where´s the onion?*) = Где је лук?

Gde je klub? (*Where´s the club?*) = Где је клуб?

Kuda? – Tamo. (*Where to? – There.*) = Куда? – Тамо.

Kako je Bora? (*How´s Bora?*) = Како је Бора?

Gde je rum? (*Where is rum?*) = Где је рум?

Ratko je u hotelu. (*Ratko is in the hotel.*) = Ратко је у хотелу.

Ta ideja je dobra i hrabra. (*This idea is good and brave.*) = Та идеја је добра и храбра.

Gora Tara je mala? (*The mountain Tara is small?*) = Гора Тара је мала?

Borka treba dobar obrok. (*Borka needs a good food portion.*) = Борка треба добар оброк.

Moje rame je belo. (*My shoulder is white.*) = Моје раме је бело.

Hotel „Bor" je dobar hotel. (*Hotel „ Bor" is a good hotel.*) = Хотел ”Бор” је добар хотел.

Borko je dobar tata. (*Borko is a good dad.*) = Борко је добар тата.

Kada je rok? (*When is the deadline?*) = Када је рок?

3. Write in Latin in your notebook or on a piece of paper and read aloud! – Napiši na latinici i čitaj glasno!

Тамо је мала хала. (*Over there is a small hall.*) = Tamo je mala hala.

Која је мера? (*What is the measure?*) = Koja je mera?

Ту је рода. (*Here is a stork.*) = Tu je roda.

Дара је мала. (*Dara is small.*) = Dara je mala.

Мато је лекар. (*Mato is a doctor.*) = Mato je lekar.

Та беба је јако лака. (*This baby is very light.*) = Ta beba je jako laka.

Та лутка је добра. (*This doll is good.*) = Ta lutka je dobra.

Вела боја је лепа боја. (*White color is a nice color.*) = Bela boja je lepa boja.

То је моје млеко. (*This is my milk.*) = To je moje mleko.

Како је та драга дама? (*How is this nice lady?*) = Kako je ta draga dama?

Ратко је храбар. (*Ratko is brave.*) = Ratko je hrabar.

Где је лед? (*Where is the ice?*) = Gde je led?

Та тема је добра. (*This theme is good.*) = Ta tema je dobra.

Тај део је добар. (*This part is good.*) = Taj deo je dobar.

Лола је у клубу. (*Lola is at the club.*) = Lola je u klubu.

Моја мама је у граду. (*My mom is in town.*) = Moja mama je u gradu.

5. lekcija

1. Write in Cyrillic in your notebook or on a piece of paper and read aloud! – Napiši na ćirilici i čitaj glasno!

idem (*I go*) = идем

keks (*cookie*) = кекс

dati (*to give*) = дати

rasti (*to grow*) = расти

barem (*at least*) = барем

Rada = Рада

jabuka (*apple*) = јабука

orah (*walnut*) = орах

program = програм

hektar (*hectare*) = хектар

istorija (*history*) = историја

Zora = Зора

meso (*meat*) = месо

izgled (*look*) = изглед

hartija (*paper*) = хартија

patos (*groud*) = патос

so (*salt*) = со

med (*honey*) = мед

sos (*sauce*) = сос

znati (*to know*) = знати

uzeti (*to take*) = узети

stati (*to stop*) = стати

hteti (*to want*) = хтети

brati (*to pick*) = брати

ukrasti (*to steal*) = украсти

jagoda (*strawberry*) = јагода

Lidija = Лидија

lek (*medicine*) = лек

gram = грам

niko (*no one*) = нико

jeka (*echo*) = јека

sladoled (*ice cream*) = сладолед

Radojka = Радојка

rad (*work*) = рад

sto (*table*) = сто

biber (*pepper*) = бибер

riba (*fish*) = риба

dinar = динар

zeleno (*green*) = зелено

zato (*therefore*) = зато

red (*order*) = ред

zabluda (*error*) = заблуда

na (*on*) = на

sa (*with*) = са

Ines = Инес

hijena (*hyena*) = хијена

dim (*smoke*) = дим

jela (*fir*) = јела

inat (*definace*) = инат

jednak (*same*) = једнак

zbog (*because*) = због

nada (*hope*) = нада

smog = смог

do (*until, up to*) = до

za (*for*) = за

tigar = тигар

eho (*echo*) = ехо

lila (*purple*) = лила

hrast (*oak*) = храст

lud (*crazy*) = луд

2. Write in Cyrillic in your notebook or on a piece of paper and read aloud! – Napiši na ćirilici i čitaj glasno!

ja sam (*I am*) = ја сам

ti si (*you are*) = ти си

on/ona/ono je (*he/she/it is*) = он/она/оно је

mi smo (*we are*) = ми смо

vi ste (*you are*) = ви сте

oni/one/ona su (*they are*) = они/оне/она су

3. Write in Cyrillic in your notebook or on a piece of paper and read aloud! – Napiši na ćirilici i čitaj glasno!

jedan (1), tri (3) = један (1), три (3)

sedam (7), osam (8), deset (10) = седам (7), осам (8), десет (10)

jedanaest (11), trinaest (13) = једанаест (11), тринаест (13)

sedamnaest (17), osamnaest (18) = седамнаест (17), осамнаест (18)

trideset (30), sedamdeset (70), osamdeset (80), sto (100) = тридесет (30), седамдесет (70), осамдесет (80)

4. Write in Cyrillic in your notebook or on a piece of paper and read aloud! – Napiši na ćirilici i čitaj glasno!

Koji je danas dan? (*What day is today?*) = Који је данас дан?

Danas je subota. (*Today is Saturday.*) = Данас је субота.

Koji je sutra dan? (*What day is tomorrow?*) = Који је сутра дан?

Sutra je utorak. (*Tomorrow is Tuesday.*) = Сутра је уторак.

Kada idemo da beremo jagode? (*When are we going to pick strawberries?*) = Када идемо да беремо јагоде?

Idemo na izlet? (*Are we going on a trip?*) = Идемо на излет?

Znati ko dolazi – to je dobro. (*Who´s coming – that´s good to know.*) = Знати ко долази – то је добро.

Mogu da dobijem keks? (*Can I have a cookie?*) = Могу да добијем кекс?

Ona je uzela jaja, meso i ribu. (*She took eggs, meat and fish.*) = Она је узела јаја, месо и рибу.

Mogu da ti dam sladoled. (*I can give you an ice cream.*) = Могу да ти дам сладолед.

U redu? (*All right?*) = У реду?

Gde stajemo? Kod restorana? (*Where do we stop? At the restaurant?*) = Где стајемо? Код ресторана?

Kako tvoje dete brzo raste! (*How fast is your child growing!*) = Како твоје дете брзо расте!

Hteli ne hteli, ali mala Radojka je sada velika. (*Whether we want it or not, but little Radojka is big now.*) = Хтели не хтели, али мала Радојка је сада велика.

Ah, barem da imaju malo nade! (*Oh, if they had at least a little hope!*) = Ах, барем да имају мало наде!

Molim te, stani! (*Stop, please!*) = Молим те, стани!

Gde rastu tako lepe zelene jabuke? (*Where do such beautiful green apples grow?*) = Где расту тако лепе зелене јабуке?

Mi nismo hteli ni ribu ni sos uz ribu. (*We wanted neither fish nor the sauce with the fish.*) = Ми нисмо хтели ни рибу ни сос уз рибу.

Ne, mala Rada nije ukrala lila hartiju. (*No, little Rada didn´t steal te purple paper.*) = Не, мала Рада није украла лила хартију.

Ko je tu lud? (*Who is crazy here?*) = Ко је ту луд?

Zbog Lidije nisi hteo mleko? (*Because of Lidija you dind´t want milk?*) = Због Лидије ниси хтео млеко?

Oni su gledali program, a mi nismo. (*They watched the program, but we didn´t.*) = Они су гледали програм, а ми нисмо.

Kada si dao lek Borku? (*When did you give the medicine to Borko?*) = Када си дао лек Борку?

To nije niti jedan gram! (*This is not even a gram!*) = То није нити један грам!

5. Write in Latin in your notebook or on a piece of paper and read aloud! – Napiši na latinici i vežbaj čitanje!

Ми добро знамо историју. (*We know very well the history.*) = Mi dobro znamo istoriju.

Нико није тако леп као Лола и Матеј. (*No one is as beautiful as Lola and Matej.*) = Niko nije tako lep kao Lola i Matej.

Зора је на аеродрому и стоји код таксија. (*Zora is at the airport and stands by the cab station.*) = Zora je na aerodromu i stoji kod taksija.

Јека у хали је једнака као јека у мојој соби. (*The echo in the hall is the same as the one in my room.*) = Jeka u hali je jednaka kao jeka u mojoj sobi.

Ми не једемо месо. (*We don´t eat meat.*) = Mi ne jedemo meso.

Ја радо узимам сладолед за десерт. (*I like having an ice cream for dessert.*) = Ja rado uzimam sladoled za desert.

Је ли изглед битан? (*Is the look important?*) = Je li izgled bitan?

Радојка има велики зелени сто. (*Radojka has a big green table.*) = Radojka ima veliki zeleni sto.

Рад је лаган ако знамо како да радимо. (*The work is easy if we know how to do it.*) = Rad je lagan ako znamo kako da radimo.

На патосу је један динар. (*There is a dinar on the floor.*) = Na patosu je jedan dinar.

И зато не идемо на море? (*And that´s why we don´t go to the sea?*) = I zato ne idemo na more?

Где су со и бибер? (*Where are the salt and papper?*) = Gde su so i biber?

Да, морамо да узмемо и мед. (*Yes, we have to take honey too.*) = Da, moramo da uzmemo i med.

Ко једе рибу? (*Who eats the fish?*) = Ko jede ribu?

Који смог у граду! (*What a smog in the town!*) = Koji smog u gradu!

Молим кекс уз какао! (*A cookie and the cocoa, please!*) = Molim keks uz kakao!

Где су сада тигар и хијена? (*Where are the tiger and hyena how?*) = Gde su sada tigar i hijena?

Реда мора бити! (*There must be order!*) = Reda mora biti!

Ти си у заблуди. (*You are under a mistake.*) = Ti si u zabludi.

Од Београда до Бора није далеко. (*It´s not far from Belgrade to Bor.*) = Od Beograda do Bora nije daleko.

Е сад не идем с тобом! (*And now I´m not going with you!*) = E sad ne idem s tobom!

Који дуги ехо! (*What a long echo!*) – Koji dugi eho!

Ја знам како изгледају храст и јела. (*I know what the oak and the fir look like.*) = Ja znam kako izgledaju hrast i jela.

Не идемо јер дим је јак. (*We are not going because the smoke is strong.*) = Ne idemo jer dim je jak.

   Snežana Stefanović: Learn Serbian Cyrillic

1. Write in Cyrillic in your notebook or on a piece of paper and read aloud! – Napiši na ćirilici i čitaj glasno!

Супермаркет ”Тезга”

радно време од девет до двадесет

затворено сваку другу суботу

Нова роба сваки дан!

Избор као у бајци!

Храна, алкохол, козметика и остале добре ствари!

Имамо и цигарете и новине!

Врхунски квалитет!

Добре цене!

Девет локација у Београду!

Близу трамвајске станице!

С нама је угодно!

Ми увек имамо времена!

Види и узми!

Supermarket „Counter"

opening hours from 9 to 20

closed every second Saturday

New goods every day!

The selection like in a fairy tale!

Food, alcohol, cosmetics and other good stuff!

We also have cigarettes and newspapers!

Top quality!

Good prices!

9 stores in Belgrade!

Near a streetcar station!

With us it is pleasant!

We always have time!

Come and take it!

2. Write in Cyrillic in your notebook or on a piece of paper and read aloud! – Napiši na ćirilici i čitaj glasno!

У ресторану

Конобарица: - Добар дан! Изволите.

Цвета: - Добар дан! Имате слободан сто за двоје?

Конобарица: - Наравно. Овде је сто.

Цвета: - Хвала. Имате сладолед? Мој син воли да једе сладолед.

Конобарица: - Да, имамо сладолед од ваниле и јагода.

Цвета: - Јовице?

Јовица: - Молим сладолед од ваниле.

Цвета: - Онда молим један сладолед од ваниле за мог Јовицу и један сладолед од јагода за мене.

Конобарица: - У реду.

In the restaurant

Waitress: - Good afternoon! Yes, please?

Cveta: - Good afternoon! Do you have a free table for two?

Waitress: - Of course. Here is the table.

Cveta: - Thank you. Do you have ice cream? My son likes ice cream.

Waitress: - Yes, we have ice cream with vanilla and strawberries.

Cveta: - Jovica?

Jovica: - I would like ice cream with vanilla.

Cveta: - Then we would like a vanilla ice cream for my Jovica and an ice cream with strawberries for me.

Waitress: - Very well.

3. Write in Latin in your notebook or on a piece of paper and read aloud! – Napiši na latinici i čitaj glasno!

Ponosni tate

Tata 1: - Moja Vukica voli matematiku.

Tata 2: - Ah da? To je interesantno. Moja Gorica ne voli matematiku, ali voli hemiju. To je skoro isto za mene. Mislim, brojevi su i tu i tamo.

Tata 1: - Ne, to nije isto. Matematika je matematika, a hemija je hemija.

Tata 2: - Gorica voli ne samo hemiju nego i biologiju. Zgodno, zar ne?

Tata 1: - Zgodno? Da?

Tata 2: - Da bude lekarka treba hemiju i biologiju.

Proud dads

Dad 1: - My Vukica likes mathematics.

Dad 2: - Really? That's interesting. My Gorica doesn't like mathematics, but she likes chemistry. It's almost the same for me. I mean, the numbers are both here and there.

Dad 1: - No, it's not the same. The math is math and the chemistry is chemistry.

Papa 2: - Gorica likes not only chemistry, but also biology. Nice, isn't it?

Papa 1: - Nice?

Papa 2: - To become a doctor she needs chemistry and biology.

4. Write in Latin in your notebook or on a piece of paper and read aloud! – Napiši na latinici i čitaj glasno!

Koncert

Milica: - Idemo na koncert?

Borivoje: - Na koji koncert?

Milica: - Vlado Georgijev ima koncert u subotu.

Borivoje: - Stvarno?

Milica: - Da.

Borivoje: - To je lepa muzika. Ja veoma volim takvu muziku, volim balade. A karte za koncert?

Milica: - Vuk ima nekoliko karata i zove nas da idemo na koncert.

Borivoje: - Super! Gde je koncert?

Milica: - U koncertnoj Sali Sava Centar.

Borivoje: - Ne znam tu lokaciju. Ja sam tek od nedavno u Beogradu. Da pogledamo na mapi?

Milica: - Ne treba. Vuk zna gde je koncertna dvorana Sava Centra. A i ja znam.

Borivoje: - Onda nazovi Vuka!

Milica: - Naravno!

Concert

Milica: - Are we going to the concert?

Borivoje: - Which concert?

Milica: - Vlado Georgijev has concert on Saturday.

Borivoje: - Really?

Milica: - Yes.

Borivoje: - This is beautiful music. Yes, I like this kind of music, I like ballads. And the tickets?

Milica: - Vuk has some tickets and invites us to the concert.

Borivoje: - Great! Where is the concert?

Milica: - In the concert hall of Sava Centar.

Borivoje: - I don't know this location. I've been in Belgrade only since the other day. Should we look in the city map?

Milica: - We don't need to. Vuk knows where the concert hall is.

Borivoje: - Then call Vuk!

Milica: - Of course!

7. lekcija

1. Write in Cyrillic in your notebook or on a piece of paper and read aloud! – Napiši na ćirilici i čitaj glasno!

После одмора

Продан, Растко, Синиша и Душан су опет у Србији. Продан је из Ниша, Растко је из Новог Сада, Синиша је из Крушевца, а Душан је из Новог Пазара.

И неколико другарица су поново у Србији. Чедомирка је из Суботице, Павлија је из Кикинде, Пелагија је из Деспотовца, Подгорка је из Крагујевца, а Душица је из Смедерева.

After vacation

Prodan, Rastko, Siniša and Dušan are back in Serbia. Prodan is from Niš, Rastko is from Novi Sad, Siniša is from Kruševac and Dušan is from Novi Pazar.

And some friends are back in Serbia. Čedomirka comes from Subotica, Pavlija comes from Kikinda, Pelagija comes from Despotovac, Podgorka comes from Kragujevac and Dušica comes from Smederevo.

2. Write in Cyrillic in your notebook or on a piece of paper and read aloud! – Napiši na ćirilici i vežbaj čitanje!

Miloš = Милош

Uroš = Урош

Borislav = Борислав

Boško = Бошко

Velko = Велко

Veselin = Веселин

Vidoje = Видоје

Vladan = Владан

Vladislav = Владислав

Gvozden = Гвозден

David = Давид

Oliver = Оливер

Radivoje = Радивоје

Raša = Раша

Sava = Сава

Vojimir = Војимир

Cvetin = Цветин

Jevrem = Јеврем

Petruška = Петрушка

Vukasin = Вукасин

Velinka = Велинка

Vera = Вера

Jelisaveta = Јелисавета

Olivera = Оливера

Savka = Савка

Dubravka = Дубравка

Lepa = Лепа

Svetlana = Светлана

Spasenija = Спасенија

Pava = Пава

Pauna = Пауна

Perka = Перка

Persa = Перса

Petra = Петра

Gaša = Гаша

Vujadin = Вујадин

Gavrilo = Гаврило

Spira = Спира

Jakov = Јаков

Poleksija = Полексија

3. Write in Cyrillic in your notebook or on a piece of paper and read aloud! – Napiši na ćirilici i vežbaj čitanje!

Obrenovac = Обреновац

Jagodin = Јагодин

Loznica = Лозница

Lazarevac = Лазаревац

Babušnica = Бабушница

Sremska Mitrovica = Сремска Митровица

Šabac = Шабац

Sombor = Сомбор

Kostolac = Костолац

Vršac = Вршац

Majdanpek = Мајданпек

Svilajnac = Свилајнац

Leskovac = Лесковац

Aleksandrovac = Александровац

Velika Plana = Велика Плана

Dimitrovgrad = Димитровград

Kladovo = Кладово

Negotin = Неготин

Sevojno = Севојно

Umka = Умка

Crvenka = Црвенка

Bajina Bašta = Бајина Башта

Grocka = Гроцка

Zlatibor = Златибор

Mladenovac = Младеновац

Petrovaradin = Петроварадин

Temerin = Темерин

Šid = Шид

4. Write in Latin in your notebook or on a piece of paper and read aloud! – Napiši na latinici i čitaj glasno!

Vreme

Danas je vreme lepo. Sunce sija i nebo je vedro. Naravno, leto je. Ali sutra – sutra dolazi kiša. Tako stoji u novinama, u prognozi vremena. Ja volim kišu. Kiša je topla i ugodna. Kiša uvek ohladi vrelinu. I kad sam na moru, ja volim da pada kiša. Kiša pada, a ja se kupam u moru. Ali kiša na moru ne pada dugo. I to volim.

Weather

Today, the weather is beautiful. The sun is shining and the sky is bright. Of course, it is summer. But tomorrow - tomorrow comes the rain. That's what it says in the newspaper, in the weather forecast. I like rain. Rain in summer is warm and pleasant. The rain always cools the heat. Even when I am at the seaside, I like when it rains. It rains and I swim in the sea. But at the sea it doesn't rain for a long time. I like that too.

5. Write in Latin in your notebook or on a piece of paper and read aloud! – Napiši na latinici i čitaj glasno!

Dogovor

Gvozden: - Šta ima danas na televiziji?

Svetlana: - U pola osam je dnevnik.

Gvozden: - Znam da je dnevnik u pola osam. Ali šta ima posle?

Svetlana: - Posle je emisija „Junaci našeg doba“.

Gvozden: - Dobro. Ima li nešto drugo?

Svetlana: - Na primer?

Gvozden: - Sport.

Svetlana: - Ima. U devet je odbojka… Ali na Drugom programu je emisija o kulturi. A ja volim emisije o kulturi.

Gvozden: - I šta sada da radimo?

Svetlana: - Imam ideju. Ako ti opereš sudove, gledamo sport – ako ja operem sudove, gledamo kulturu.

Gvozden: - … Sve sudove?

Deal

Gvozden: - What's on TV today?

Svetlana: - News is on at half past 8.

Gvozden: - I know there's news at half past 8. But what's on after that?

Svetlana: - After that there is the program „The Heroes of Our Time".

Gvozden: - Good. Is there anything else?

Svetlana: - For example?

Gvozden: - Sports.

Svetlana: - Yes, there is. At 9 there is volleyball... But in the Second Program there is a cultural program. And I like cultural programs.

Gvozden: - And what should we do now?

Svetlana: - I have an idea. If you wash the dishes, then we'll watch the sports program - if I do it, we'll watch the cultural program.

Gvozden: - ... All the dishes?

8. lekcija

1. Write in Cyrillic in your notebook or on a piece of paper and read aloud! – Napiši na ćirilici i čitaj glasno!

a) Telefoni u Srbiji: = Телефони у Србији:

policija – jedan devet dva = **полиција – један девет два**

vatrogasci – jedan devet tri = ватрогасци – један девет три

tačno vreme – devet pet = тачно време – девет пет

brojevi telefona – devet osam osam = **бројеви телефона – девет осам осам**

vojna policija – devet osam šest nula = војна полиција – девет осам шест нула

---

b) Govorni automati su: = Говорни аутомати су:

- pravoslavni verski praznici i običaji – devet osam dva dva

православни верски празници и обичаји – двет осам два два

- meteorološki podaci – devet osam dva tri

метеоролошки подаци – двет осам два три

- loto i sportska prognoza – devet osam četiri četiri

лото и спортска прогноза – девет осам четири четири

a) Telephone numbers in Serbia:

Police – 192

Fire department – 193

Time (What time is it?) – 95

Phone book – 988

Military police – 9860

b) Language machines:

Orthodox holidays and customs – 9822

Weather information – 9823

Lotto and sports betting – 9844

2. Write in Cyrillic in your notebook or on a piece of paper and read aloud! – Napiši na ćirilici i vežbaj čitanje!

Srpska jela = *Serbian dishes* = Српска јела

sarma od kiselog kupusa = *meat roulade with sour cabbage* = сарма од киселог купуса

paradajz čorba = *thick tomato soup* = парадајз чорба

pogača s blitvom = *salty cake with chard* = погача с блитвом

ajvar od zelenog paradajza = *ajvar (vegetable spread) with green tomatoes* = ајвар од зеленог парадајза

pogača s tikvicama = *salty cake with zucchini* = погача с тиквицама

kolač s muskatnom tikvom = *cake with muscat pumpkin* = колач с мускатном тиквом

srpska čorba od mesa = *Serbian thick meat soup* = српска чорба од меса junetina s pečurkama = *young beef with mushrooms* = јунетина с печуркама

vinski paprikaš od somovine = *wine goulash with catfish* = вински паприкаш од сомовине

pržena jaja sa slaninom = *fried eggs with bacon* = пржена јаја са сланином

zapečena boranija = *baked white beans* = запечена боранија

pastrmka u vinu = *trout in wine* = пастрмка у вину

belo meso u pavlaci = *white meat in sour cream* = бело месо у павлаци

sarma od slatkog kupusa = *meat roulade with sweet cabbage* = сарма од слатког купуса

kiseli feferoni = *pickled pepperoni* = кисели феферони

biftek = *beefsteak* = бифтек

fiš-paprikaš = *goulash with fish* = фиш-паприкаш

3. Write in Latin in your notebook or on a piece of paper and read aloud! – Napiši na latinici i čitaj glasno!

Živan i Jefimija su muž i žena skoro deset godina. = *Živan and Jefimija are husband and wife for almost 10 years.*

Čedomirka i Ružica su sestre i žive u Nišu. = *Čedomirka and Ružica are sisters and live in Niš.*

Filipa i Blaženka su drugarice i idu na kafu. = *Filipa and Blaženka are friends and go for a coffee.*

Snežana i Božidarka su komšinice i vole fudbal. = *Snežana and Božidarka are neighbors and like soccer.*

Živomir i Nadežda su brat i sestra i vole da igraju šah. = *Živomir and Nadežda are siblings and like to play chess.*

Želimirka i Momčilo idu u bioskop svaku subotu. = *Želimirka and Momčilo go to the cinema every Saturday.*

Živka i Časlavka studiraju filozofiju. = *Živka and Časlavka study philosophy.*

Filotej i Sofija idu u osnovnu školu. = *Filotej and Sofija attend elementary school.*

Božana i Živana su profesorke na univerzitetu. = *Božana and Živana are professors at the university.*

4. Write in Latin in your notebook or on a piece of paper and read aloud! – Napiši na latinici i čitaj glasno!

U Srbiji možete da posetite fantastične lokale i restorane, dobre pabove i lokale s modernom muzikom kao i tradicionalne kafane. Čitav dan možete da kupujete u veoma interesantnim i dobrim mestima za šoping. Želite da vidite znamenitosti Srbije? Možete da posetite manastire i crkve – oni su važni deo srpske kulture i tradicije. Isto tako možete da odete u muzeje i galerije u svim gradovima. U gradovima možete da uživate u barovima, možete da otkrijete čari beogradskih splavova i da posetite čarobne klubove. Ako želite da naučite srpski jezik, možete da upišete tečaj srpskog jezika. Ako tražite ekskluzivan gradski hotel ili želite da odsednete u etno selu, i u tome možete da uživate u Srbiji.

In Serbia you can visit fantastic pubs and restaurants, good bars and places with modern music, but also traditional coffee houses. All day, you can shop in very interesting and good shopping places. Would you like to visit the sights of Serbia? You can visit monasteries and churches - they are an important part of Serbian culture and tradition. Likewise, you can go to museums and galleries in all cities. In the cities you can enjoy the bars, discover the charm of Belgrade float locales and visit enchanting clubs. If you want to learn Serbian language, you can enroll in a course of Serbian language. Are you looking for an exclusive hotel or do you want to spend time in an ethnic village, you can enjoy that too in Serbia.

5. Read aloud! – Čitaj glasno!

forum, futur, čaj, fokus, čembalo, farsa, anemičan, flaša, antipatičan, forma, Žaklina, fizika, Figaro, Ruža, fakat, artičoka, finale, čili, fosil, Fanija, fusnota, figura, Filipa, folija, faktor, Živadinka, fešta, palačinka, fuzija, funta, Živanka, fijaker, forte, familija, žirafa, famozan, praktičan, fanatik, žiri, farma, fenomen, definitivno, farmer, fasciniran, delfin, fatalan, flora, fauna, filozofija, federacija, festival, folklor, figurativan, tajfun, film, Živoslava, filter, finalist, tarifa, finiš, firma, trijumf, formular, Živkica, funkcija, biografija

1. Write in Cyrillic in your notebook or on a piece of paper and read aloud! – Napiši na ćirilici i čitaj glasno!

jagnjetina s pasuljem = *lamb with beans* = јагњетина с пасуљем

srpske ćufte = *Serbian meatballs* = српске ћуфте

pljeskavica na srpski način = *Serbian style minced loaf* = пљескавица на српски начин

riblja čorba = *fish soup* = рибља чорба

svinjski ražnjići sa žalfijom = = *pork skewers with sage* = свињски ражњићи са жалфијом

pirinač s povrćem = *rice with vegetables* = пиринач с поврћем

proja sa spanaćem = *salty semolina cake with spinach* = проја са спанаћем

žuti pasulj s govedinom = *yellow beans with beef* = жути пасуљ с говедином

teleća kisela čorba = *sour thick beef soup* = телећа кисела чорба

keleraba sa ćuftama = *cabbage abi with meatballs* = келераба са ћуфтама

paprike punjene lignjama = *peppers stuffed with kalmari* = паприке пуњене лигњама

svinjetina u sosu od ajvara = *pork in ajvar sauce* = свињетина у сосу од ајвара

ražnjići od piletine sa sosom od oraha = *chicken skewers in walnut sauce* = ражњићи од пилетине са сосом од ораха

kisele paprike punjene sirom = *pickled peppers stuffed with cheese* = кисele паприke пуњене сиром

pasulj na starinski način = *beans in traditional way* = пасуљ на старински начин

mešani pileći ražnjići = *mixed chicken skewers* = мешани пилећи ражњићи

2. Write in Cyrillic in your notebook or on a piece of paper and read aloud! – Napiši na ćirilici i čitaj glasno!

Детињство

Ја се добро сећам мојих школских другара и другарица. Мој најбољи друг се звао Љубомир Пресановић. Он је седео са мном у клупи и сви су га звали Љуба. Ја сам увек играо с њим и са Смиљаном фудбал на великом одмору. Да је Смиљана играла с нама фудбал, није било необично: кад смо деца, онда нема разлике – сви се играмо заједно. Смиља је била заљубљена у Драгољуба. Њега смо звали Драган и он је био најбољи ученик у разреду. Он је седео са

Жељком у клупи и они су били заљубљени. Много девојчица у разреду су биле заљубљене у Драгана. Посебно Босиљка, Миља и Дуња. У Босиљку, Миљу и Дуњу су били други дечаци заљубљени: у Босиљку је био заљубљен Љуба, у Миљу је био заљубљен Огњен, а у Дуњу је био заљубљен Немања. Кад је у разред дошао Угљеша Перић, онда се све променило. И љубав, и другарство и фудбал. Заправо не знам да ли се све променило због Угљеше Перића или зато што смо сви дошли у пубертет.

Childhood

I remember my school friends well. My best friend was called Ljubomir Presanović. He sat next to me on the school bench and everyone called him Ljuba. I used to play soccer with him and Smiljana during the school break. Smiljana playing soccer with us was not unusual: when you are a child, there is no difference - everyone plays together. Smilja was in love with Dragoljub. We called him Dragan and he was the model student in the class. He sat next to Željka on the school bench and they were in love with each other. Many girls in the class were in love with Dragan. Especially Bosiljka, Milja and Dunja. Other boys were in love with Bosiljka, Milja and Dunja: Ljuba was in love with Bosiljka, Ognjen was in love with Milja, and Nemanja was in love with Dunja. When Uglješa Perić came to the class, everything changed. Both love and friendship and soccer. Actually, I don't know if everything changed because of Uglješa Perić or because we all went through puberty.

3. Write in Latin in your notebook or on a piece of paper and read aloud! – Napiši na latinici i čitaj glasno!

Radnja mojeg oca

Ja se zovem Ćanka Dražić i ja živim u Dorćolu. Dorćol se nalazi u centru Beograda. Moji roditelji imaju malu staru kuću gde sam ja odrasla. Naša kuća ima prizemlje, prvi i drugi sprat. Mi živimo na prvom i drugom spratu, a u prizemlju kuće moj otac ima radnju. On je krojač u trećoj generaciji. On uglavnom radi opravke odeće za svoje stalne mušterije. Čak i nedeljom. Iako on ne može da puno zaradi i iako ima veliku konkurenciju u skupim radnjama, on voli svoj posao.

My father's store

My name is Ćanka Dražić and I live in Dorćol. Dorćol is located in the center of Belgrade. My parents have a small old house where I grew up. Our house has the ground floor, the first floor and the second floor. We live on the first and second floor, and on the ground floor my father has his store. He is a tailor in the third generation. He mostly does clothing repairs for his regular customers. Even on Sundays. Although he can't earn much and although he faces a lot of competition from expensive stores, he likes his job..

---

4. Write in Latin in your notebook or on a piece of paper and read aloud! – Napiši na latinici i čitaj glasno!

Banje u Srbiji

U Srbiji su banje veoma omiljene. Vrnjačka Banja je veoma lepa banja i ima čak sedam izvora lekovite vode. Sokobanja je isto tako lepa banja i njene vode su dobre protiv astme i disajnih problema. Banja Koviljača ili Kraljevska banja ima bogatu istoriju i dugu tradiciju u lečenju osteoporoze i reume. Niška Banja je jedna od najpopularnijih banja u Srbiji i njeni lekarski timovi su odlični u dijagnostici. Ovčar Banja je u centru netaknute prirode i njena voda ima trideset osam stepena. Banja Kanjiža se nalazi u Vojvodini i njene vode su neverovatno tople – između pedeset i sedamdeset stepena.

Spas in Serbia

Spas are very popular in Serbia. Vrnjačka Banja is a very nice spa and has even 7 springs of medicinal water. Sokobanja is also a beautiful spa and its water is good for asthma and for respiratory problems. Banja Koviljača or Royal Spa has a rich history and long tradition in treatment of osteoprosis and rheumatism. Niška Banja is one of the most popular spas in Serbia and its medical teams are excellent in diagnostics. Ovčar Banja is located in the middle of untouched nature and its water is 38 degrees hot. Banja Kanjiža is located in Vojvodina and its water is incredibly warm - between 50 and 70 degrees.

10. lekcija

1. Write in Cyrillic in your notebook or on a piece of paper and read aloud! – Napiši na ćirilici i vežbaj čitanje!

Која јела волимо?

Ја волим ђувеч. Моја мама воли пилећу џигерицу. Мој тата воли леђну сланину. Моја старија сестра Рађа воли колаче са смеђим шећером. Мој млађи брат Ђорђе воли грожђе и колаче који се зову медвеђе шапе. Моја тетка Анђелка воли чорбу од медвеђег лука. Моја стрина Ђурђа воли сок од ђумбира. Мој стриц Ђуро воли сва јела с патлиџаном. Моја баба Анђа воли џем од шљива и џем од кајсија.

What dishes do we like?

I like đuveč (stew of vegetables, meat and rice). My mom likes chicken liver. My dad likes back bacon. My older sister Rađa likes cakes with brown sugar. My younger brother Đorđe likes grapes and the cake called „ bear paws". My aunt Anđelka likes thick wild garlic soup. My aunt Đurđa likes ginger juice. My uncle Đuro likes all dishes with melanzani. My grandma Anđa likes plum jam and apricot jam.

2. Write in Cyrillic in your notebook or on a piece of paper and read aloud! – Napiši na ćirilici i vežbaj čitanje!

Moja sestra

Моја сестра се зове Ђулијана и ја је јако волим. Али оно што ја не волим код ње јесте њено тражење ствари по кући. У суботу је, на пример, цео дан тражила своје смеђе ђинђуве. На крају их је нашла, али и ја сам морао да тражим те ђинђуве. Али – морам да признам – и она мени помаже код домаћих задатака па је фер да и ја њој понекад помажем. Али прекјуче је опет била потрага за њеним стварима – за пиџамом. Она је рекла: ”Ђурице, буди џентлмен и помози дами у невољи.” Тако сам и ја тражио пиџаму. И нашли смо пиџаму у џаку за стару одећу. Како је она тамо дошла, ја то не знам. Сада тражимо њен џемпер и чизме. Ђулијана је рекла да ћу да добијем пола њеног џепарца ако их нађем.

My sister

My sister's name is Đulijana and I love her very much. But the thing I don't like with her is her searching for things through the apartment. On Saturday, for example, she was looking for her brown earrings all day. Finally she found them, but I had to look for those earrings too. But - I have to admit - she also helps me with homework, so it's fair that I also help her sometimes. But the day before yesterday there was also another search for her things - for her pajamas. She said, „ Đurica, be a gentleman and help the lady in need." So, I was also looking for the pajamas. And we found the pajamas in a bag of old clothes. How it got there, I don't know. Now we are looking for her sweater and boots. Đulijana said that I will get half of her pocket money when I find it.

3. Write in Latin in your notebook or on a piece of paper and read aloud! – Napiši na latinici i vežbaj čitanje!

Oglas

Izdajemo mali nameišteni dvosobni stan u Beogradu sa centralnim grejanjem. Stan je nov i u blizini je autobuska stanica i pijaca. U kvartu se nalazi također i engleski koledž Džordž Bajron kao i osnovna škola. Stan iznajmljujemo i porodicama i studentima.

Advertisement

We rent a small furnished apartment in Belgrade with central heating. The apartment is new and nearby there is bus stop and vegetable market. In the neighborhood there is also the English University George Byron, as well as an elementary school. We rent the apartment both to families and students.

4. Write in Latin in your notebook or on a piece of paper and read aloud! – Napiši na latinici i vežbaj čitanje!

Ćevabdžinica „Veseli ćevapi"

U ulici Džordža Vašingtona otvorena je ćevabdžinica „Veseli ćevapi". Vlasnik ćevabdžinice je inženjer Đuro Đorđević i gospođa Đurđica Samardžić. Nova ćevabdžinica ima na ponudi klasične ćevape i lokal je veoma ugodan. Kad smo pitali zašto se njihova radnja zove „Veseli ćevapi", gospodin Đorđević je rekao: „Kad vidim deset malih ćevapa na tanjiru, onda oni izgledaju za mene kao mala vesela deca. Zato se naša radnja zove „Veseli ćevapi".

Snack store for ćevapi (minced meat rolls) called „Funny ćevapi"

The snack store for ćevapi was opened in Georg Washington Street. The snack shop owner is engineer Đuro Đorđević and Mrs. Đurđica Samardžić. The new snack store has in its offer classic ćevapi (minced meat rolls) and the place is very cozy. When we asked why the store is called „Funny ćevapi", Mr. Đorđević said: „When I see 10 little ćevapi on the plate, they look like little funny kids to me. That's why our store is called „Funny ćevapi".

5. Write in Latin in your notebook or on a piece of paper and read aloud! – Napiši na latinici i vežbaj čitanje!

Telefonski brojevi = *Telephone numbers*

Hitna pomoć – jedan devet četiri = *Rescue service – 194*

Vojna hitna pomoć – devet sedam šest = *Military rescue service – 976*

Prijava telefonskih smetnji – devet sedam sedam = *Telephone troubleshooting – 977*

Pomoć na putu – devet osam sedam = *Roadside assistance – 987*

Služba buđenja – devet osam jedan jedan = *Wake-up service by telephone – 9811*

Razna obaveštenja – devet osam jedan dva – *Miscellaneous information – 9812*

11. lekcija

1. Read aloud! – Vežbaj čitanje!

definitivno	disketa	pidžama
kandidat	cigareta	admiral
papagaj	paradajz	katedrala
gramatika	digresija	dijamant
meteorologija	vaga	dresura
arheologija	dinosaurus	kondor
fudbal	bas	bife
šofer	diskusija	Balkan
kafa	džem	lord
bedž	magazin	rum
snob	film	džungla
grof	kugla	šminka
šunka	hokej	as
brigada	vodvilj	bal
biro	garancija	dama
garderoba	drenaža	komandir
kurir	manir	moda
model	rezerva	arija
milion	kasa	lava
salama	freska	gama

2. Read aloud! – Vežbaj čitanje!

horizont	fanatičan	kaktus
palma	ćevapčići	stepa
antilopa	biskvit	sultan
eventualno	apostol	Toronto
antipatičan	Timotije	pol
Tara	start	ekvador
nautika	banka	Pavle
fantazija	komet	sport
planet	tulipan	parola

zenit	televizija	Tihana
Tomo	astronomija	tata
Jupiter	albatros	centar
Venera	oltar	patrola
helikopter	marcipan	pab
istorija	atom	papir
bestseler	teritorij	Niš
vakuum	hijena	Saturn
tramvaj	meteorit	zebra
stop	ekran	Mars
Sibir	arsenal	komisija
baraka	frizura	kafana
kukuruz	kivi	balet
biografija	major	radio
realizacija	rakija	sardina
Barcelona	artikl	kozmonaut
Mađarska	banket	Neptun
violina	kontrabas	klavir
dirigent	policija	auto
Adam	Sokrat	intervju
duet	kompjuter	telefon
konflikt	internacionalan	puding
džemper	krompir	majstor
futrola	artiljerija	armija
Bukurešt	kanton	paraf
apoteka	kompas	salata
sirup	votka	metal

3. Read aloud! – Vežbaj čitanje!

Oglasi

Udovac (45 godina) iz Beograda, po zanimanju mehaničar, traži partnerku. Hobiji: automobili, fudbal i šetnje uz Dunav. Volim da kuvam i da se brinem o kući. Želje: brak i deca. Šifra: „Zauvek tvoj"

Udovica (35 godina) iz Niša, po zanimanju medicinska sestra, traži partnera. Nemam decu, volim da pišem poeziju. Iako pišem poeziju, nisam romantična: ne volim da šetam i da gledam zvezde po noći. Volim da igram odbojku i da izlazim. Šifra: „Život je kratak"

Advertisements

Widower *(45 years) from Belgrade, mechanic by profession, looking for a partner. Hobbies: cars, soccer and walks along the Danube. I like cooking and taking care of the household. Wishes: marriage and children. Password: „Yours forever"*

Widow *(35 years) from Niš, nurse by profession, looking for a partner. I have no children, I like to write poetry. Although I write poetry, I am not romantic: I don't like walks and looking at the stars. I like playing volleyball and going out in the evening. Password: „Life is short"*

4. Read aloud! – Vežbaj čitanje!

Perfektni dan

Danas imam slobodan dan. To je lepo. Ne moram ništa da radim. Znači: mogu da radim šta hoću. Danas mogu da pijem kafu na miru, mogu da doručkujem dugo, mogu da idem u grad. Šta mogu da radim u gradu? Mogu da posetim Mariju. Da, mogu da odem do nje i da je pitam kako je. Onda možemo da idemo zajedno na ručak. Gde na ručak? Da, to je dobro pitanje. Ali Marija sigurno zna dobre restorane. Posle ručka možemo da odemo u park, da sedimo na klupi i da pričamo. To je lepo – park u proleće. Uveče možemo da idemo u bioskop ili u pozorište. U bioskopima ima uvek dobrih filmova i u pozorištu ima uvek dobrih predstava. Posle možemo da odemo u neki noćni klub i da igramo. Ili samo da slušamo muziku. To je lepo. Imati perfektni dan.

A perfect day

Today I have a day off. That is nice. I don't have to do anything. That means: I can do what I want. Today I can drink my coffee in peace, I can have a long breakfast, I can go to town. What can I do in the city? I can visit Marija. Yes, I can go to her and ask her how she is. Then we can have lunch together. Where to have lunch? Yes, that's a good question. But I'm sure Marija knows good restaurants. After lunch we can go to the park, sit on the bench and talk. It's beautiful - the park in spring. In the evening we can go to the cinema or the theater. In cinemas there are always good movies and in theaters there are always good shows. After that we can go to a club and dance. Or just listen to the good music. That's nice. To have a perfect day.

5. Read aloud! – Vežbaj čitanje!

Citati

Moj sin se zove Timotije i ima pet godina. On ima veoma zanimljive misli i ja moram da ga citiram. On kaže na primer:

Danas nema sunca jer se sunce još nije probudilo.

Moja baka je debela jer ona nosi puno reči u sebi.

Ja volim da idem u zološki vrt jer tamo mogu da vidim majmune koji se smeju ljudima.

Moj tata ponekad komplikuje moju mamu, a moja mama ponekad ne razume šta moj tata govori.

Ja volim da idem na selo kod babe Dare jer ona ima kokoške koje su prirodne.

Quotes

My son's name is Timotije and he is five years old. He has very interesting thoughts and I have to quote him. For example, he says:

Today there is no sun because the sun has not woken up yet.

My grandma is fat because she has many words in her.

I like to visit the zoo because there I can see monkeys laughing at people.

My dad sometimes complicates my mom, and my mom sometimes doesn't understand what my dad says.

I like to go to the village to grandma Dara because she has hens that are natural.

6. Read aloud! – Vežbaj čitanje!

Poruke

Na stolu leži poruka od Petra:

Dolazim za pet minuta. Zašto ne radi tvoj mobilni telefon?

Nakon deset minuta Gordana čita poruku i piše poruku:

Ja idem kod frizera. Dolazim za tri časa. Ne znam zašto ne radi moj mobilni.

Nakon tri sata Petar piše poruku:

Gde si? Ne javljaš se na mobilni. Ja sada idem kod mehaničara. Dolazim za dvadeset minuta.

Nakon trideset minuta Gordana piše poruku:

Zašto sada ne radi tvoj mobilni? Kada dolaziš? Ja moram da idem u školu zbog

Dragana, danas je roditeljski sastanak. Dolazimo kući posle pet.

U šest Petar piše poruku:

Gde ste? Ja ne volim da pišem poruke na hartiji ako već svi imamo mobitele. Idem na trening. Dolazim oko osam.

U deset Gordana piše poruku:

Gde si? Večera je na stolu, ja spavam. Sutra sam ceo dan na konferenciji. A ti?

Messages

There is a message from Petar on the table:

I'll be there in 5 minutes. Why is your cell phone not working?

After 10 minutes Gordana reads the message and writes a message:

I'm going to the hairdresser. I will be back in three hours. I don't know what's wrong with my cell phone.

After three hours Petar writes the message:

Where are you? You don't answer your cell phone. I'm going to the mechanic now. I will be back in 20 minutes.

After 30 minutes Gordana writes the message:

Why is your phone not working now? When will you be back? I have to go to school because of Dragan, today is parents' evening. We are home after 5.

At 6 Peter writes a message:

Where are you? I don't like to write messages on paper when we all have cell phones already. I'm going to my training. I will be back around 8.

At 9 Gordana writes the message:

Where are you? Dinner is on the table, I am sleeping. Tomorrow I'll be in a conference all day. And you?

12. lekcija

2. Write in written letters in your notebook or on a piece of paper and read aloud! – Napiši na pisanoj ćirilici i vežbaj čitanje!

galaksija = *галаксија* muzika = *музика*

agava = *агава* smog = *смог*

ada = *ада*

akacija = *акација*

Indija = *Индија*

geografija = *географија*

menza = *менза*

bambus = *бамбус*

vikend = *викенд*

banda = *банда*

deo = *део*

hiljada = *хиљада*

agrar = *аграр*

aukcija = *аукција*

decidiran = *децидиран*

dresura = *дресура*

kadifa = *кадифа*

konkavan = *конкаван*

oralan = *оралан*

vezir = *везир*

majka = *мајка*

Sava = *Сава*

ekologija = *екологија*

alkohol = *алкохол*

huligan = *хулиган*

Ilija = *Илија*

soda = *сода*

jubilej = *јубилеј*

civilizacija = *цивилизација*

masovno = *масовно*

ajvar = *ајвар*

bilans = *биланс*

digresija = *дигресија*

imigracija = *имиграција*

konfuzija = *конфузија*

musaka = *мусака*

rival = *ривал*

Danska = *Данска*

3. Write in written letters in your notebook or on a piece of paper and read aloud! – Napiši na pisanoj ćirilici i vežbaj čitanje!

Draga Gordana! = *Драга Гордана!*

Draga Dunja! = *Драга Дуња!*

Draga Smiljana! = *Драга Смиљана!*

Dragi Njegoslave! = *Драги Његославе!*

Dragi Dragoljube! = *Драги Драгољубе!*

Dragi Ljubo! = *Драги Љубо!*

4. Write in written letters in your notebook or on a piece of paper and read aloud! – Napiši na pisanoj ćirilici i vežbaj čitanje!

afinitet = афинитет

amortizer = амортизер

bagatela = багатела

desert = десерт

citadela = цитадела

plasman = пласман

duplikat = дупликат

emigrant = емигрант

entitet = ентитет

evidentno = евидентно

fundament = фундамент

gabarit = габарит

insekt = инсект

integritet = интегритет

intencija = интенција

intenzitet = интензитет

irelevantan = ирелевантан

notoran = ноторан

kontradiktoran = контрадикторан

opsesija = опсесија

orbita = орбита

plafon = плафон

proces = процес

pumpa = пумпа

pompa = помпа

relevantan = релевантан

rabat = рабат

spontano = спонтано

striktan = стриктан

šansona = шансона

šank = шанк

tendencija = тенденција

terakota = теракота

tirada = тирада

trik = трик

vijadukt = вијадукт

vinjeta = вињета

šarlatan = шарлатан

kompot = компот

viski = виски

5. Write in written letters in your notebook or on a piece of paper and read aloud! – Napiši na pisanoj ćirilici i vežbaj čitanje!

Poštovani gospodine Markoviću! = *Поштовани господине Марковићу!*

Poštovana gospođo Perić! = *Поштована госпођо Перић!*

Poštovani gospodine Vladiću! = *Поштовани господине Владићу!*

Poštovana gospođo Jovanović! = *Поштована госпођо Јовановић!*

poštovani = honored

6. Write the text in your notebook or on a piece of paper and read it loud! – Prepiši tekst i vežbaj čitanje!

Meseci u godini su: januar, februar, mart, april, maj, juni, juli, avgust, septembar, oktobar, novembar i decembar.

Months in the year are: January, February, March, April, May, June, July, August, September, October, November and December.

Dana u nedelji su: ponedeljak, utorak, sreda, četvrtak, petak, subota i nedelja.

Days in the week are: Monday, Tuesday, Wednesday, Thursday, Friday, Saturday and Sunday.

Godišnja doba su: proleće, leto, jesen i zima.

Seasons are: spring, summer, autumn and winter.

7. Write the text in written script in your notebook or on a piece of paper! – Prepiši tekst pisanim slovima!

Нови филм

Данило: - Идемо данас у биоскоп?

Мила: - Добра идеја. Шта гледамо?

Данило: - Знаш филм "Било једном у Србији"?

Мила: - Не, не знам. То је нови филм?

Данило: - Да.

Мила: - Је ли то драма?

Данило: - И драма и комедија. Критичари кажу да је то добар филм. Играју добри глумци.

Мила: - Може. Ја волим да гледам домаће филмове.

A new movie

Danilo: - Shall we go to the cinema today?

Mila: - Good idea. What are we going to watch?

Danilo: - Do you know the movie „Once Upon a Time in Serbia"?

Mila: - No, I don't know it. That's a new movie?

Danilo: - Yes.

Mila: - Is it a drama?

Danilo: - Both drama and comedy. The critics say that this is a good movie. There are good actors and actresses playing.

Mila: - All right. I like domestic film productions.

Answer the questions in written script in your notebook or on a piece of paper! – Odgovori pismeno koristeći ćirilična pisana slova!

1. Ko ide u bioskop? = *Who goes to the cinema?* – **Мила и Данило.** (*Mila and Danilo.*)

2. Koji je film u bioskopu? = *What movie is playing in the theater?* – **"било једном у Србији".** (*„Once Upon a Time in Serbia")*

3. Je li to novi film? = *Is this a new movie?* – **Да, то је нови филм.** (*Yes, this is a new movie.*)

4. Je li film drama ili komedija? = *Is the movie a drama or a comedy?* – **Филм је и драма и комедија.** (*The movie is both a drama and a comedy.*)

5. Šta kažu kritičari za film? = *What do the critics say about the film?* – **Критичари кажу да је филм добар.** (*The critics say that the movie is good.*)

6. Ko igra u filmu? = *Who is acting in the movie?* – **У филму играју добри глумци и глумице.** (*There are good actors and actresses in the movie.*)

7. Da li Mila voli da gleda domaće filmove? = *Does Mila like domestic film productions?* – **Да.** (*Yes.*)

8. Read and answer the questions in your notebook or on a piece of paper! – Čitaj i odgovori na pitanja!

Idemo u pozorište

Smiljana: - Hoćemo u pozorište?

Vuk: - Naravno. To želimo već dugo. Šta ima na repertoaru?

Smiljana: - „Gospođa ministarka" igra u Narodnom pozorištu.

Vuk: - Odlično. Ja volim Branislava Nušića. On je moj omiljeni pisac.

Smiljana: - I moj.

Vuk: - Kada su predstave?

Smiljana: - U subotu je premijera.

Vuk: - Onda idemo u subotu.

We are going to the theater

Smiljana: - Shall we go to the theater?

Vuk: - Of course. We have wanted to for a long time. What is on the repertoire?

Smiljana: - „ Mrs. Minister " is playing in the Folk Theater.

Vuk: - Very good. I like Branislav Nušić. He is my favorite author.

Smiljana: - Mine too.

Vuk: - When are the shows?

Smiljana: - On Saturday is the premiere.

Vuk: - Then we 'll go on Saturday.

Pitanja:

1. Da li Smiljana i Vuk žele već dugo da idu u pozorište? = *Have Smiljana and Vuk wanted to go to the theater for a long time?* – Da. (*Yes.*)

2. Šta ima na repertoaru u Narodnom pozorištu? = *Was gibt es auf dem Repertoire im Volkstheater?* – „Gospođa ministarka". (*„Frau Ministerin".*)

3. Ko voli Branislava Nušića? = *Who likes Branislav Nušić?* – Vuk i Smiljana vole Branislava Nušića. (*Vuk and Smiljana like Branislav Nušić.*)

4. Kada je premijera? = *When is the premiere?* – Premijera je u subotu. (*The premiere is on Saturday.*)

---

5. Da li Smiljana i Vuk idu na premijeru? = *Are Smiljana and Vuk going to the premiere? – Da. (Yes.)*

9. Read and answer the questions in your notebook or on a piece of paper! – Čitaj i odgovori na pitanja!

Kako izgleda moja učiteljica?

Moja učiteljica se zove Zvezdana i ona je mlada. Ona ima dugu smeđu kosu i plave oči. Ona je visoka i vitka. Moja učiteljica često nosi košulje i pantalone. Ponekad nosi suknju. Moja učiteljica se često smeje i zato ja volim moju učiteljicu.

What does my teacher look like?

My teacher's name is Zvezdana and she is young. She has long brown hair and blue eyes. She is tall and slim. My teacher often wears shirts and pants. Sometimes she wears a skirt. My teacher often laughs and that is why I like my teacher.

Pitanja:

1. Kako se zove njegova učiteljica? = *What is the name of his teacher?* – Ona se zove Zvezdana. (*Her name is Zvezdana.*)

2. Je li ona stara? = *Is she old?* – Ne, ona nije stara, ona je mlada. (*No, she is not old, she is young.*)

3. Kakvu kosu ima Zvezdana? = *What kind of hair does Zvezdana have?* – Ona ima dugu smeđu kosu. (*She has long brown hair.*)

4. Kakve su njene oči? = *What are her eyes like?* – Njene oči su plave. (*Her eyes are blue.*)

5. Je li ona niska? = *Is she short?* – Ne, ona je visoka. (*No, she is tall.*)

6. Je li ona vitka ili punašna? = *Is she slim or chubby?* – Ona je vitka. (*She is slim.*)

7. Šta često nosi Zvezdana? = *What does Zvezdana often wear?* – Zvezdana često nosi košulje i pantalone. (*Zvezdana often wears shirts and pants.*)

8. Šta ponekad nosi Zvezdana? = *What does Zvezdana wear sometimes?* – Zvezdana nosi ponekad suknju. (*Zvezdana sometimes wears a skirt.*)

9. Zašto on voli učiteljicu Zvezdanu? = *Why does he like the teacher Zvezdana?* – On voli Zvezdanu jer se ona često smeje. (*He likes Zvezdana because she often laughs.*)

10. Write the text in Latin script in your notebook or on a piece of paper and read it aloud! – Prepiši tekst na latinicu i čitaj glasno!

Znam ćirilicu!

Šta sada mogu? Sada mogu da čitam knjige, novine i na internetu različite sajtove. Mogu da pišem mejlove i sms-ove. Mogu da čitam nazive ulica i nazive prodavnica bez problema. Mogu čak da pišem moj privatni dnevnik na ćirilici. Mogu da napišem i knjigu na ćirilici. To je interesantno jer ja već dugo skupljam ideje za moju knjigu. Ali ne želim odmah da pišem na ćirilici nego tek posle.

Ovo su moje ideje:

- *Moj junak se zove Lukas. On je profesor geografije i voli da putuje. Kao ja.*

- *On želi da poseti Srbiju jer tamo ima rodbinu. Zašto? Njegova mama je iz Srbije.*

- *Šta je njegov problem? On ne zna srpski i ne zna ćirilicu. To nije veliki problem jer rodbina zna engleski. Njegov problem je što on želi da ide svake godine u Srbiju. Dakle, on treba srpski i ćirilicu.*

- *On želi da upozna Beograd, Novi Sad i Niš.*

To je sve od ideja. Zasada.

Ah, da! Ovo je ideja od danas, zapisao sam je na cedulji:

- *Moj Lukas treba da upozna devojku. Ona se zove Sonja. Ona isto voli da putuje kao Lukas. Ali ona želi da upozna Evropu. To je problem za Lukasa. Šta Lukas može da napravi? Može da putuje sa Sonjom po Evropi ili da ostane u Srbiji.*

Da, to su moje ideje. Ali te ideje već mogu da pišem i na latinici i na ćirilici.

I can write Cyrillic!

What can I do now? I can read books, newspapers and websites. I can write emails and text messages. I can read street names and store addresses with ease. I can even keep my private daily journal in Cyrillic. I can also write a book in Cyrillic. This is interesting because I have been collecting the idea for my book for a long time. But I don't want to write in Cyrillic right away, but later.

These are my ideas:

- My hero's name is Luke. He is a geography professor and likes traveling. So do I.

- He wants to visit Serbia because he has relatives there. Why? Because his mother is from Serbia by origin.

- What is his problem? He doesn't know Serbian and doesn't know the Cyrillic script. This is not a big problem because his relatives know English. His problem is that he wants to visit Serbia every year. So he needs Serbian and Cyrillic.

- He wants to know Belgrade, Novi Sad and Niš.

That's all from the ideas. For now.

Oh, yes! This is today's idea, written on a piece of paper:

- My Lukas should meet a young woman. Her name is Sonja. She also likes traveling, like Lukas. But she wants to get to know Europe. This is a problem for Lukas. What can Lukas do? He can either travel around Europe with Sonja or stay in Serbia.

Yes, these are my ideas. But I can write this idea both in Latin script and in Cyrillic script.

10. Write the whole „azbuka" in Cyrillic: block letters, block letters in cursive and written letters! – Napiši azbuku na ćirilici – štampana slova, štampana kosa slova i pisana slova!

AZBUKA

	A	B	V	G	D
Block letters	А а	Б б	В в	Г г	Д д
Block letters in cursive	*А а*	*Б б*	*В в*	*Г г*	*Д д*
Written letters	*А а*	*Б б*	*В в*	*Г г*	*Д д*

	Đ	E	Ž	Z	I
Block letters	Ђ ђ	Е е	Ж ж	З з	И и
Block letters in cursive	*Ђ ђ*	*Е е*	*Ж ж*	*З з*	*И и*
Written letters	*Ђ ђ*	*Е е*	*Ж ж*	*З з*	*И и*

	J	K	L	Lj	M
Block letters	Ј ј	К к	Л л	Љ љ	М м
Block letters in cursive	*Ј ј*	*К к*	*Л л*	*Љ љ*	*М м*
Written letters	*Ј ј*	*К к*	*Л л*	*Љ љ*	*М м*

	N	Nj	O	P	R
Block letters	Н н	Њ њ	О о	П п	Р р
Block letters in cursive	*Н н*	*Њ њ*	*О о*	*П п*	*Р р*

Written letters	Н н	Њ њ	О о	П п	Р р

	S	T	Ć	U	F
Block letters	С с	Т т	Ћ ћ	У у	Ф ф
Block letters in cursive	С с	Т т	Ћ ћ	У у	Ф ф
Written letters	С с	Т т	Ћ ћ	У у	Ф ф

	H	C	Č	Dž	Š
Block letters	Х х	Ц ц	Ч ч	Џ џ	Ш ш
Block letters in cursive	Х х	Ц ц	Ч ч	Џ џ	Ш ш
Written letters	Х х	Ц ц	Ч ч	Џ џ	Ш ш

Serbian Reader

Updated August 2023

Reading Books

A1 = Novice Low / Mid / High

Snežana Stefanović: IDEMO DALJE 1 – Reading Book
paperback, e-book, audiobook, interactive e-book with audio

Snežana Stefanović: Trifun i mali fudbaleri – Short Story
paperback, e-book

Snežana Stefanović: IDEMO DALJE 2 – Reading Book
paperback, e-book, audiobook, interactive e-book with audio texts

A2 = Intermediate Low

Snežana Stefanović: IDEMO DALJE 3 – Reading Book
paperback & e-book

Snežana Stefanović: Serbian: Jokes and Anecdotes, Part 1
paperback & e-book

Snežana Stefanović: Serbian: Jokes and Anecdotes, Part 2
paperback & e-book

B1 = Intermediate Mid / High

Snežana Stefanović: IDEMO DALJE 4 – Reading Book
paperback & e-book

C1 = Advanced High

Snežana Stefanović: VREME – Short Stories
paperback & e-book

Textbooks

A1 = Novice Low / Mid / High

Snežana Stefanović: Serbian: Vocabulary Practice A1 to the Book "Idemo dalje 1"
paperback & e-book

Snežana Stefanović: Serbian: Simple Sentences 1
paperback, e-book, audiobook, interactive e-book with audio

Snežana Stefanović: Serbian: Simple Sentences 2
paperback & e-book

Snežana Stefanović: Learn Serbian Cyrillic
paperback & e-book

Visit our website

www.serbian-reader.com

and learn more about the series „Serbian Reader IDEMO DALJE" as well as

about continuous publication of new books